Thames & Hudson

WATERSIDE
MODERN

DOMINIC **BRADBURY**

PHOTOGRAPHS BY RICHARD **POWERS**

400+ ILLUSTRATIONS

CONTENTS

ICONIC WATERSIDE **HOUSES**

The draw of the ocean is inevitable and irresistible. It is as though there is some innate need in all of us to find our way, every now and then, to the water's edge in search of the restorative power of the sea. We may be searching for very different things, yet from childhood onwards that sense of fascination is always with us. The sea and the waterways of the world exert a strong and enduring influence upon us all.

For some, the water represents a source of sustenance and trade, a way of making a mark upon the world; for others, it is a perpetual siren of indulgence. The Victorians, in particular, turned seaside enjoyment into a unique industry, creating the idea of pleasure piers, where day-trippers and holiday makers would relax and recharge. The coast was seen as a place of health and vitality, with a 'rest cure' by the sea becoming a common theme in nineteenth-century society.

The sea and the great waterways have also been a key source of artistic inspiration. From painters to poets, the ocean has been a rich and constant siren, as it has been for the great storytellers. So many of the most captivating stories feature the sea as an essential character in the drama, from Homer's *Odyssey* to Herman Melville's *Moby-Dick*, Ernest Hemingway's

The Old Man and the Sea to William Golding's *Rites of Passage* and Yann Martel's *Life of Pi*. Joseph Conrad, Charles Dickens, Daphne du Maurier and many others have drawn the ocean into their work and made the sea into a stage.

For architects and designers, too, the shoreline is both an enduring temptation and a powerful setting in which to build. It requires a particular sensitivity to and respect for the natural beauty of the surroundings, usually well protected by planning constraints, and creating a home in such a context carries a special responsibility. Yet clearly the rewards can be extraordinary. Even an urban river setting has a definite allure, offering architects the opportunity to create a building with a sense of connection to an enigmatic thoroughfare that offers light, calm and a rhythmic natural beauty.

Many landmark houses of the twentieth century have a waterside setting. They include such influential buildings as Casa Malaparte (1941), designed by architect Adalberto Libera for the novelist Curzio Malaparte, and perched on a rocky peninsula on the island of Capri. When architect and client fell out, Malaparte continued the project alone, creating one of the most dramatic waterside houses of the twentieth century.

Other key exemplars include Paul Rudolph's Milam Residence (1962) in Florida, Staffan Berglund's futuristic Villa Spies (1969) on the Swedish island of Torö and Antti Lovag's sinuous Palais Bulles (1975–89), near Cannes, built for fashion designer Pierre Cardin. The Arango House (1973), one of John Lautner's most engaging and sculptural buildings, overlooks the Pacific at Acapulco, Mexico, and Can Lis (1971), built by Jørn Utzon at Porto Petro, Majorca, has a collection of indoor and outdoor rooms tied directly to the ocean vista. In each case, the architecture was guided by the relationship to the sea, as well as by the constraints of the site itself.

In 1951, Le Corbusier famously built a small timber cabin for himself and his wife at Roquebrune-Cap-Martin, in the south of France. Despite the modesty of the house, a vivid contrast to the sophistication and complexity of so many of his buildings, the architect often suggested that this is where he was at his happiest and at his most creative. The cabin stands next door to Eileen Gray's E-1027 (1929), a highly influential modernist villa with decks overlooking the water, which lend the house the poetic echoes of an ocean liner.

The dream of living by the sea, then, has a long and engaging history. But building by the ocean has always been a demanding process. Clifftop sites can be steep and uneven,

requiring a bespoke solution and careful engineering. Flood risk may well be a serious consideration on low-lying sites, while building materials must be carefully chosen for their resilience to the sea spray. Some materials, such as brick, can be eaten away by the salty air, and softwoods are susceptible to the extreme weather that can be a feature of waterside living.

The extremes of coast and shore – as with mountain homes – make the design and construction of waterside buildings a special case. The most successful of these are those that seek to work with the setting, to the point that the land and sea become visually integrated with the indoor and outdoor living spaces of the house. These are, by necessity and desire, highly contextual and respectful buildings, which respond to the specific conditions, light and landscape to create something that is organic and tailored, as well as considered and refined.

Frank Lloyd Wright famously argued for just this kind of site-sensitive approach, where the architecture of a building is a thoughtful reaction to the conditions and topography of the landscape, as well as to the needs of the client. At Fallingwater (1939), in southwestern Pennsylvania, Wright arranged terraces around the flow of Bear Run, a stream running through the site, with parts of the building pushed out over it, in response to the client's love of the landscape and the sound of the waterfalls.

Scott Tallon Walker's landmark Goulding Summerhouse (1972) in Ireland offers another dramatic but very different response to a riverside setting, with a floating rectangular structure of steel, glass and timber that cantilevers in dramatic fashion out over the River Dargle.

It is the combination of natural beauty and a desire to be at the water's edge that drives the dream of waterside living, even when the challenges involved are demanding. River and ocean frontages are prime locations in so many of the world's great cities, offering not just a waterside vista, but also the refreshing sense of space and the rich quality of light that comes with such open settings. Coastal homes and waterside communities have a resonance that consistently engages us, especially when they have a distinct and imaginative character all of their own.

One thinks of the beachside cabin and garden at Dungeness, in Kent, England, that was the home of artist and film-maker Derek Jarman, or the Californian community of Sea Ranch, which represented a conscious attempt in the 1960s to create an oceanside community with a modernist spirit and an eco-conscious sensibility. Or perhaps Andrew Geller's quirky, sculpted mid-century beach houses on Long Island, designed with a light and imaginative touch, and given such nicknames as the 'Milk Carton' and the 'Butterfly'.

Indeed, there is a significant common thread to the best waterside homes: an ecological sensitivity and awareness, combined with a true sense of depth and character. It is the natural beauty of these ocean and riverside sites that sparks the initial ambition to build a home at the water's edge. The ambition has to be to frame the view and enhance the sense of connection with the surroundings, while seeking to respect and preserve the natural environment as much as possible. It is just such a sensitivity, advocated by Wright and others, that characterizes the waterfront houses in this book. They represent the dream of modern waterside living, combined with a perpetual love of the sea.

'Whenever I find myself growing grim about the mouth; whenever it is a damp, drizzly November in my soul...I quietly take to the ship...,' says Ishmael in *Moby-Dick*. 'There is nothing surprising in this. If they but knew it, almost all men in their degree, some time or other, cherish very nearly the same feelings towards the ocean with me.'

Most of us, men and women, can see some truth in Ishmael's words. The sea and the shoreline make for strange kinds of sirens. They do call us. And it makes the dream of waterside living a constant temptation and a profound delight.

BEACH
HOUSE

BEACH HOUSE

The most enticing beach houses are always defined by a sense of freedom. There is a casual informality to beachside living and an openness to the sea, as well as to themes of restorative pleasure, escapist indulgence and intimate interaction with nature. Time by the beach seems to be different from time spent anywhere else, helping to add to that welcome feeling of liberation.

'Time is more complex near the sea than in any other place,' wrote John Steinbeck in *Tortilla Flat*, 'for in addition to the circling of the sun and the turning of the seasons, the waves beat out the passage of time on the rocks and the tides rise and fall as a great clepsydra.'

The best beach houses are infused with a free spirit and are places of friendly informality where the usual restrictions of daily working life are put on hold. They often serve as second homes and holiday retreats, lifted by an open design approach that suits this kind of sanctuary but might feel out of place in the city. This approach also promotes a sense of connection with the sea, leading the eye ever outwards. These homes offer a choice of outdoor living spaces on terraces, decks and balconies, each with a unique perspective on the natural surroundings.

A beach house at Amagansett, on Long Island (p. 24), by Yabu Pushelberg has viewing points and outdoor rooms that connect with the views and surrounding dunes. The same is true of Casa MTL (p. 66), Bernardes Arquitetura's house in Laranjeiras, on Brazil's Atlantic coast, where you can walk directly onto the beach and into the water without passing through a clutter of fences, gates and walls. The beach becomes part of the house, creating the perfect outdoor room, crafted by nature.

The beach house has a long and varied history, from the thatched *palapas* of Mexico and Latin America to the simple fishermen's huts of England and France. There is a wide variety to the shape, form and conception of traditional beachside dwellings, but common to them all is a feeling of simplicity. Many are just a single storey in height, and made with easily available materials. They often have a sense of impermanence and vulnerability that is endearing, although sometimes challenging in extreme weather. They are a modest and discreet presence upon the coastline.

Today, the contemporary beach house is designed to be enduring, as well as sustainable. But rather than drawing inspiration from Victorian seaside villas or imposing coastal

fortresses, these modern dwellings look to buildings that, in Glenn Murcutt's phrase, 'touch the earth lightly', seeking a direct and intimate connection with the coast and the sea. In some parts of the world, particularly England and parts of Europe, beachside cabins have become known as chalets, sharing a natural, organic character with their timber-built mountain cousins. These waterside huts stand in stark contrast to the vast oceanfront developments that have overwhelmed many popular coastal communities.

The best modern beach houses are characterized by an imaginative approach and a sensitivity to land and sea. Modernist pioneer Andrew Geller may never have expected his quirky timber huts on Long Island to last more than a few decades, but many have survived to become desirable and much-loved residences. On Shelter Island, at Long Island's southern tip, designer Jonathan Adler created a beachside enclave in collaboration with architectural firm Gray Organschi, which has a refreshing spirit and rich personality (p. 34). And the house that architect Carlos Ferrater designed for his brother on the Costa del Azahar, in Spain, is full of charm, character and individuality, with only a grove of palm trees between the house and the beach (p. 76).

Certain picturesque coastal communities around the world have been defined by their beach houses. Dungeness in Kent, England, has become known the world over for its row of former fishermen's cabins, which now attract architects and artists, tempted by an extraordinary seascape and the shingle beach. This is the location for Johnson Naylor's beach house on the site of an old maritime experimental station (p. 56), close to one of the town's two lighthouses.

It is, of course, the location that drives the design of these houses. From Piet Boon's vision for a house in Bonaire (p. 44) to Fearon Hay's Dune House in Omaha, New Zealand (p. 14), these are buildings that seek to connect with the landscape and embrace that sense of intimacy with the sea. Modernity, geometry, sensitivity and contextuality are the key ingredients of contemporary beach houses that frame the view and blur the boundaries between indoors and out, as well as between land and sea.

It is this sense of intimacy that is so vital to the individual character of the beach house. The relationship with the ocean is immediate and powerful, and the sound of the rolling surf is a constant companion and a source of inspiration. The sense of freedom in such places is palpable.

DUNE HOUSE

FEARON HAY ARCHITECTS OMAHA, NEW ZEALAND

Undulating duneland forms a soft blanket that wraps around Fearon Hay's Dune House, on the eastern coast of New Zealand's North Island. The natural beauty of this hinterland between house and sea forms a dramatic backdrop to a building conceived with thoughtful sensitivity to its surroundings. The design responds to views out to the open sea, while naturalistic landscaping ensures that the low-slung building fits into the setting with the lightest of touches.

The house was commissioned by a couple from Auckland, about an hour's drive away, who wanted a house that they could use regularly, rather than simply as a weekend or holiday home. The building was designed around their needs and the location, but also with an awareness of the occasional breezes that blow in from the ocean and the issue of privacy. Views of the neighbouring houses were to be avoided, meaning that the building had to be focused largely on the open vista of the shore and the sea beyond, where dolphins are a familiar sight.

'The house looks due east over the water, and has angled views of the headlands along the coast,' says architect Jeff Fearon. 'It is a spectacular setting, an important factor when thinking about the floor levels and ensuring connections with the views. The sun comes from behind in the afternoon, but as there are a number of neighbours both behind and next to the house, we included glass screens around a courtyard to allow in the afternoon sun while still retaining privacy.'

A modest lower level includes a garage and a guest suite, as well as the entrance, from which you step up onto the main floor and into the house proper. Here, you find yourself in the courtyard, protected by walls of semi-opaque glass, which protect this sheltered outdoor room, complete with a monolithic outdoor fireplace, a dining zone and a pool

The view from the pool and courtyard through the main living space to the dunes and the ocean beyond (*opposite*). The master suite also offers an open vista, looking out to the open water (*below*); the four-poster bed is a custom piece by Penny Hay.

to one side, pushed up against the glass walls. An olive tree planted at
one end of the pool and a frangipani in a large planter by the fireplace
add additional notes of green to the filtered colours of the dunes passing
through the glass. A wall of floor-to-ceiling glass slides away to open
the courtyard up to the main living area; another wall retreats at the
other end of the room, opening out to a terrace that faces the open vista.

This open-plan living space combines kitchen, dining and seating
areas, with the dining table positioned to make the most of the sea view.
The kitchen is a custom design by the architects, with units fronted in
a warm, glowing brass metallic finish that offers a welcome contrast to
the concrete floor and palette of soft greys throughout. The architects
collaborated on the interiors both with the clients and with interior
designer Penny Hay, who designed a number of bespoke pieces of
furniture for the house. The vintage French chandelier above the
dining table adds an unexpected touch. Here and in the master
bedroom, alongside the main living area, wraparound linen curtains
can be used to cocoon the spaces, helping to soften and dissolve the
linear character of the architecture.

The indoor-outdoor relationship is maximized in the master suite,
where the windows slide back to open onto a balcony; clear glass
balustrades ensure that the view is uninterrupted. The clients' outdoor
lifestyle is catered for throughout, with outdoor showers for use when
coming back from the beach and storage lockers for surf boards and
other equipment. It is a tailored house, tied to the setting and subtly
nestled within it. The glass screens also give the house an enigmatic
quality, like an artwork installation placed carefully upon the dunes.

GROUND-FLOOR PLAN

SECTION

A glass screen around the courtyard and
pool provides privacy without blocking
out natural light (*opposite*); the front of the
building is open to the view (*above*), with a
terrace adjoining the main living spaces.

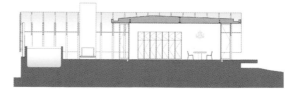

The open-plan living area includes the kitchen, dining area and a lounge zone; the sofas are by Flexform and the dining table is a bespoke piece by Penny Hay in oak and brass (*left*). The custom kitchen (*above*) has brass finishes for both the island and fitted units.

The master bedroom opens out onto a private terrace (*opposite, top left*), while the master bathroom features a vintage French mirror. A recessed gas fireplace forms a focal point for the seating area (*above*); the 'Eva' armchair in the living room (*opposite, bottom right*) is by Vittorio Bonacina.

The planting around the pool and courtyard lends an organic element to this outdoor zone, while the soft greens of the dunes filter through the milk-glass screen.

AMAGANSETT HOUSE

YABU PUSHELBERG LONG ISLAND, NEW YORK, USA

Living by the water's edge has always held a powerful attraction for designers George Yabu and Glenn Pushelberg. Their apartment in Manhattan looks out across the Hudson River, and they have a holiday home in Miami's South Beach. Even their house in Toronto, where they first started their design studio back in the 1980s, overlooks a creek. So when they came across a 'plastic shingle-ese' house in Amagansett, on Long Island, it was not the house itself that was of interest but its enticing beachside location – the perfect spot to build a new home.

The house itself is a modestly scaled but beautifully conceived two-storey home, coated in timber and pushed into the dunes with sensitivity and care for the landscape. There are two guest bedrooms and a bunkroom on the ground floor, while the master suite and principal living spaces are on the upper level, along with the deck, to make the most of the views of the Atlantic. There is also a rooftop terrace for drinking in the scenery.

The couple shuttle back and forth between their studios in Toronto and New York, as well as travelling further afield to work on a portfolio of projects that now includes hotels and residences in Europe, Asia and North and South America, and have owned their New York apartment in a Richard Meier-designed building for a number of years. One weekend they happened to spot an advertisement in the Sunday papers for a property in Amagansett, and, having bought the site, the pair camped out at the house periodically over the next two years, getting to know the building and working out their design approach. There were a number of planning restrictions, including height and the setback from the sea, but these were seen as positive challenges. Construction took another two years.

The house forges a strong relationship with the ocean, particularly on the upper level of the house, with its elevated deck (*opposite*). An outdoor shower sits alongside the house, next to a boardwalk down to the beach (*below*).

'We tend to work quite organically,' says Pushelberg. 'When we build for ourselves we take our time, because we want to make sure that it's right for us. It was a pretty straightforward house to build, although there were a ton of restrictions. But by working with those restrictions, you create possibilities. In the end, we got a great house.'

The main living spaces on the upper level are arranged around the views of the ocean, with a custom fireplace forming a focal point. Beyond is a dining zone, while the bespoke kitchen is separated from the rest of the space by a striking steel-framed 'shopfront' window. Organic materials, such as the timber panelling and oak floors, lend the interiors a real sense of warmth. The floorboards were heat-treated in an oven to deepen the colour and lend them a more irregular texture, while the retractable glass walls are partially protected by sliding timber screens, which form a brise soleil and soften the outline of the building.

The blend of furniture includes a number of pieces from Avenue Road, the furniture retail company that the couple co-founded with Stephan Weishaupt, and vintage treasures designed by Joaquim Tenreiro and others. Although modestly sized, the house offers a good choice of different places to sit, eat and relax, including outdoor areas, such as the elevated deck and a sheltered veranda at ground level, complete with a barbecue, a dumbwaiter that connects to the upstairs kitchen and a large outdoor table.

The house makes for an idyllic retreat from the pressures of a busy and international work schedule. For the couple, Amagansett is a place to escape to and relax within an enclave that is much quieter and calmer in character than many other parts of the Hamptons.

FIRST-FLOOR PLAN

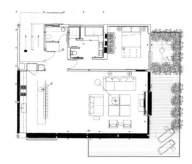

GROUND-FLOOR PLAN

Sliding timber screens form a brise soleil to provide shade and privacy as needed; they also help protect the building when not in use and provide an organic note of warmth.

The seating area on the upper level is arranged around the view and the bespoke fireplace (*right*). Sliding glass walls retract for a sense of connection with the deck and the ocean. The 'Kimono' sofa was designed by Frigerio; the leather armchair (*above*) is a vintage campaign chair.

The master suite (*above*) is on the upper level of the house, while the lower level features a bunkroom (*above right*), two guest bedrooms (*opposite*) and a separate media room. The sliding timber louvres can be used in place of the sliding windows to offer natural ventilation, while also providing privacy and security.

The lower storey incorporates an outdoor lounge and dining room, with integrated kitchenette and bar (*opposite*); the dining table and benches are from Van Rossum. The main seating zone on the upper level features armchairs by Joaquim Tenreiro and a coffee table by Jaehyo Lee (*top right*).

SEASIDE HOUSE

JONATHAN ADLER / GRAY ORGANSCHI SHELTER ISLAND, NEW YORK, USA

Set within the waters of Gardiners Bay and cradled by the outstretched northern and southern forks of Long Island, Shelter Island has a unique character all of its own. Compared to the pace of life in the Hamptons – just a short ferry ride away – Shelter Island feels much more relaxed and tranquil. This is a place to escape to and unwind. No wonder, then, that designer and potter Jonathan Adler and his partner Simon Doonan, writer and Creative Ambassador-at-Large for Barneys department stores, have been coming out here for the last twenty years.

Originally the couple spent weekends and holidays away from their Manhattan apartment at a small, A-frame house dating from the 1960s, before an irresistible opportunity arose to buy a plot of land right next to the sea, looking out to Orient Point and its coffee-pot lighthouse on the tip of the north fork. With yachts tacking across the water and the gentle rhythm of the ocean, it was an ideal place to build a new home.

The pair knew from the outset that they wanted something very different from the grand beach mansions in the Hamptons. The house needed to be informal and casual, fitting the character of the place and harking back to the simple mid-century beach cabins of Fire Island, as well as drawing inspiration from the house Adler grew up in: his parents' modernist, Scandinavian-style home, which has proved a key influence on his work ever since. There is also a hint of the courtyard houses of Japan, where Doonan spends a good deal of time for Barneys, consulting on the look of the group's Japanese stores.

Approaching the single-storey house, which was designed in collaboration with architects Gray Organschi, the first thing you see is an enigmatic barrier of black timber pierced by a double gate, with echoes of Japanese-style charcoal walls. Stepping through the gate, you find yourself in a courtyard garden, complete with a breakfast

The house looks out to Orient Point across the waters of Gardiners Bay. The positioning of the house makes the most of the vista, with a series of outdoor rooms arranged around the swimming pool and the waterside elevation of the building.

nook to one side. In front of you is an orange front door – an entryway into a world that is distinctly Adler's.

Beyond the entrance hall is a generous, open space, lightly separated into four distinct seating areas in each corner; in the centre sits a dramatic bespoke fireplace with a conical hood. Rugs, chairs and ceramics of Adler's own design are mixed with mid-century classics by Warren Platner and others within a trademark combination of pattern, texture, colour and exuberance, infused with a retro spirit of optimistic playfulness. To one side of the sitting room, there are a couple of steps up to the dining area and the kitchen, with display shelves and surfaces packed with Adler's ceramics.

Adler designed many bespoke pieces especially for the house, including a screen formed of rounded, sculpted blocks of aerated cement, which helps to separate the entrance hall from the rest of the main living space, as well as the beautifully crafted, textured tiles that form a backdrop in the kitchen and line the wall of one corner of the sitting room. The pattern reappears on the outer wall of the veranda, which is positioned for best appreciating the views of the lighthouse and provides a choice spot for fresh-air dining.

The bespoke tiles reappear in the master bedroom, over the bed, which is orientated to the ocean view. There are also two guest bedrooms and a modest gym; outside, the swimming pool is positioned at right angles to the ocean, with a pool pavilion alongside. The landscaping, designed by Vickie Cardaro, is low key but full of rich textures, with evergreens mixed with grasses and circular stepping stones interspersed with seashells gathered from the beaches.

FLOOR PLAN

SECTION

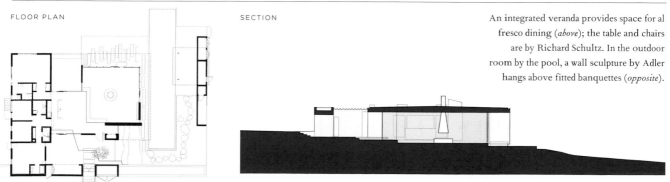

An integrated veranda provides space for al fresco dining (*above*); the table and chairs are by Richard Schultz. In the outdoor room by the pool, a wall sculpture by Adler hangs above fitted banquettes (*opposite*).

The main living area features a bespoke
screen in aerated concrete that separates
off the entrance hall and a bespoke
sofa, also by Adler (*left*). The kitchen and
dining zones are subtly demarcated with
a shift in floor level (*above*); the mural on
the island is by John-Paul Philippe.

Other seating areas are defined by focal
points including the fireplace, the fitted
library and a corner wall of custom tiles.
Much of the furniture in the space is by
Adler, with some mid-century pieces
by Warren Platner, Geoffrey Harcourt
and others thrown into the mix.

The bedrooms and bathrooms are full
of colour, pattern, texture and playful
touches. The master bedroom (*above
and left*) features a wood burner in fire-
engine red next to a vintage Dunbar sofa
upholstered in a Jack Lenor Larsen-
designed fabric, while the tiles behind
the bed are another Adler design.

KAS DORRIE

PIET BOON BONAIRE, CARIBBEAN

So many aspects of daily life revolve around the sea on the Caribbean island of Bonaire. This Dutch territory, floating off the coast of Venezuela, is famous for its sea salt, beaches and coral reefs, and relies on tourists who come not just for the benign climate, but also for the scuba diving and to enjoy the waters around the island. The entire coastline of Bonaire is a protected marine sanctuary.

'The strong relationship between the house, the beach and the sea is key to a beach house,' says Dutch designer Piet Boon, who first visited the island in the early 1980s and has designed a number of houses here. 'This is one of the most enviable locations on Bonaire, where you can step down into the sea directly from the house. The owners have a private staircase into the water from their garden, and we've created a design that really optimizes the ocean view.'

The two-storey building combines a crisp, geometrical outline with a considered response to the site and the natural conditions. Materials were chosen for their hard-wearing character and resilience to the salty air, as well as for their practicality, texture and lustre. Red cedar and teak were used for the grand timber porch, ventilation louvres and the brise soleil, while the floors are in polished concrete; patios and pathways were made using locally and sustainably sourced corals.

The principal living spaces have been elevated to the upper level to make the most of the views across the ocean. They include the main sitting room, which flows out to a sheltered terrace overlooking the beach and the open water. The kitchen and a dining/breakfast area are also positioned on the top floor, along with the master bedroom. The lower level is devoted to three more bedrooms, as well as the main dining area, sitting close to a processional entrance zone, which is demarcated by a hallway with a textured floor that continues the

The two-storey house enjoys a direct relationship with the beach and the sea, which laps at the boundary wall at high tide. The building and its thatched pavilion were designed to enhance this sense of connection in every respect.

pathway from the beach and passes right through the house to the rear garden, defining a key transitional axis from inside to out.

A range of indoor-outdoor spaces and outdoor rooms are both integral and vital. They include terraces, a courtyard garden and more sheltered verandas, which provide an intersection between indoor and outdoor living. Natural ventilation is used where possible – via louvres and openings – with the exception of the air-conditioned bedrooms. The pool terrace facing the beach is another key relaxation zone, complete with a thatched gazebo overlooking the sea, which provides shade and shelter at the warmest points of the day.

'When we designed our first villa on the island, we looked at the local architecture and building materials,' notes Boon. 'So the design principles of the villa are based upon those of traditional *cunucu* houses on the island, and allow the breeze to pass through the house unhindered and provide natural ventilation. The interiors are functional and minimalist but warm, with a lot of attention to detail. The walls and ceilings are in pure white, but the subtle colours of the furniture, accessories and artwork give elegance and warmth.'

Importantly, the beach house offers a good deal of flexibility in the way that it is used and enjoyed, with a range of indoor, outdoor and in-between spaces to choose from at different times of day and according to the weather and the movement of the sun. Such a degree of choice can only enhance the experience of beachside living, with different vantage points and perspectives from which to enjoy this unique and enticing location.

FIRST-FLOOR PLAN

GROUND-FLOOR PLAN

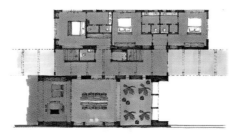

The interiors are soothing and full of light and texture. Polished concrete floors (*opposite*) contrast with natural timber and a textured hallway embedded with coral that runs through the house (*above*).

The main sitting room is situated on the upper level, facing the ocean, to make the most of the vista through the picture window (*opposite*). Much of the furniture is bespoke, designed by the architect, lending the interiors a cohesive and seamless character (*above*).

The kitchen (*opposite*) and an adjoining
breakfast room are on the upper level,
but the main dining area (*above*) is on the
ground floor, leading out to a sheltered
courtyard garden; the fitted dining table
and the chairs are by the architect.

The house includes three bedrooms on the lower level and one suite on the upper storey. All of the bedrooms feature integrated design elements, including recessed shelves, vanity units and mosquito nets.

The swimming pool and beachside area
at the front of the house feature a number
of outdoor rooms. These include seating
on the pool terrace with outdoor showers
and a thatched pavilion, which provides
shade from the midday sun and a relaxation
space a stone's throw from the sea.

EXPERIMENTAL STATION

JOHNSON NAYLOR DUNGENESS, KENT, UK

Dungeness has a particular allure for those with a creative spirit, who are so often seduced by its eclectic collection of buildings and the unique coastal landscape. The characterful shacks and cabins that stand along the coast road once belonged to fishermen; some still do, but others have been converted into holiday homes or rebuilt with striking results. One of the most famous residents, artist and film-maker Derek Jarman, created an inspirational beach garden alongside his own retreat.

The setting is certainly dramatic, enigmatic and picturesque. Dungeness is home to the largest shingle beach in Europe and is classed as Britain's only desert. Yet the area is rich in plant and birdlife, despite the extreme environment, and is a protected site of Special Scientific Interest. The elephant in the room is the nuclear power station, completed in two sections in 1965 and 1983. It is ever present yet, after a time, somehow seems to fade from consciousness.

Architect Fiona Naylor and her partner, Magnum photographer Peter Marlow, first settled in Dungeness in 2000, after Marlow visited for a newspaper assignment. He noticed that the Coastguard Tower was being vacated, and the couple made an offer on the building. They converted the tower into a family residence, but were then tempted by another opportunity next door – the Experimental Station.

The station was established by Trinity House, the body that runs and looks after most of the lighthouses in the UK, as well as providing other navigation services. Sitting close to the 1901 lighthouse, it was used for the development and testing of a range of technologies for maritime use, from foghorns to optics, photovoltaics to wind power. Eventually the station was closed, sold to a private buyer, and then sold again to the couple and Naylor's business partner, Brian Johnson.

The Experimental Station includes a number of buildings arranged on the shingle within sight of the sea. Among them are watchtowers and an old foghorn testing unit, with its distinctive black and white array.

The Experimental Station is a collection of single-storey pavilions in a compound formation, punctuated by small towers and structures. Johnson replaced some sheds towards the rear of the site with a home of his own, while Naylor and Marlow share a nearby brick building and a smaller satellite that serves as a bunkroom and playroom for their three children. A further pavilion closer to the beach is shared by everyone, and mostly used by visiting friends and family. It's an arrangement that allows for a good deal of flexibility.

The reinvention of the couple's master pavilion required a lengthy conversion process that lasted for nine months. Around 30 per cent of the bricks had spalled in the salty conditions and needed to be replaced. The interiors were completely redesigned, with three modestly sized bedrooms, a kitchen/dining room to the rear and a large sitting room to the front. This is the focal point of the building in winter, with a bespoke fireplace and a large picture window facing the sea. A sheltered area to one side, partially protected by the overhanging roofline, was turned into an outdoor room for use in warmer weather.

'On a clear night you can see the four red port lights of Calais flashing in the distance and the street lights of Wissant,' Naylor says. 'It is a brilliant place for sitting outside.'

Some time after the reinvention of the station was completed, the couple decided to rent out their original Coastguard Tower home, but could never bear to sell it. Indeed, the temptation to embark on another project here has proved too much and Naylor is now at work on two buildings just along the coast road. Dungeness is a place that draws you in, and the couple are clearly here for the long term.

Timber shutters in the guest pavilion fold down to create terraces; the two chairs are by Poul Kjærholm and Jørgen Høj (*opposite*). The original rail tracks were used for transporting equipment (*above*).

The family home has three bedrooms, an open-plan living area and a separate dining room and kitchen. A large picture window frames a view of the guest pavilion and the beach; the B&B Italia sofa is by Antonio Citterio, as is the chair by the window.

In the guest pavilion, the sleeping area is in a corner of the open-plan space (*opposite top and below*); the sofa is by Burkhard Vogtherr, the chairs are by Poul Kjærholm. The living room of the family pavilion (*opposite bottom*) has a library wall; the master bedroom is tucked away to the rear.

The dining room in the family pavilion leads out to a sheltered outdoor room, protected from the prevailing winds (*opposite*); the Cassina chair by the fire is a design by Gerrit Rietveld. The kitchen features a cook's table designed by Naylor and an Ercol love seat (*below*).

CASA MTL

BERNARDES ARQUITETURA LARANJEIRAS, RIO DE JANEIRO, BRAZIL

One of the most enticing stretches of the Brazilian coastline lies to the southwest of Rio de Janeiro, in the Serra da Bocaina National Park, where the tropical forestry of the Mata Atlântica finds its way to the coast. Not far from the picturesque colonial town of Paraty lies a small community by the sea, where Bernardes Arquitetura created a beach house for their client in the space of just seven months.

'The location is very special,' says architect Thiago Bernardes. 'Along with the sea view, you have the river junction and a waterfall, so the idea was all about bringing the natural beauty inside the house, while ensuring the family's privacy. Considering the beauty of the place, it was necessary to establish a relationship between inside and outside living spaces. The client is also an art collector, so we integrated a number of important art pieces, both inside and outside the home.'

Bernardes has known the homeowner for many years, and architect and client developed a strong bond. While the deadline of seven months was challenging, the process was helped by this spirit of understanding and a welcoming response to the proposed design ideas. Just as the site itself is unspoilt and unencumbered by any boundaries between the land, the beach and the sea, so the architecture also became a process of eroding and blurring boundaries between indoors and out.

This was partly achieved by a generous provision of outdoor rooms and living areas, all facing the ocean. An enclosed courtyard to the rear offers a more sheltered outdoor room, creating a whole series of choices about where and how to enjoy the experience of outdoor living. A veranda facing the water features an outdoor dining area, kitchenette/bar and barbecue, providing everything that might be needed for fresh-air entertaining.

A green lawn is all that separates the house from the beach and the sea. The house forges a direct relationship with the ocean via its many decks and terraces.

Another key element of the design is the transparency of the building, with floor-to-ceiling walls of glass that slide away to dissolve any separation between indoor and outdoor space. This is especially true of the main living room on the ground floor – an open-plan zone where the glass retracts to the veranda to one side and the courtyard to the other; within the room itself are spaces for sitting, relaxing and dining. At the far end, the swimming pool passes right through the building, connecting the terrace and courtyard and enhancing the sense of transparency and the notion of flexible boundaries.

'The swimming pool creates a sense of connection between the different ambiences and characters of these spaces,' says Bernardes. 'It also means that the family can use the pool without going outside if the weather is not so good.'

The main staircase sits within a double-height atrium alongside the primary entrance of the house. Upstairs are four bedrooms, with the generously scaled master suite looking out to the ocean and opening onto a private balcony and large roof terrace. Materials are warm and organic in character. Freijo and cumaru timber were used for the floors, terraces and façades, and eucalyptus for some of the structural elements; the hidden framework is in steel for strength and longevity. In the living area, floors and ceilings are in wood, while the dining area has a stone floor from the same limestone found in the entrance hallway.

With the constant sound of the waves and the sea birds calling, this is a house that truly pleases all the senses. The successful dissolution of solid walls and divisions between outside and inside further enhances the rich sensory quality of the experience of beachside living.

GROUND-FLOOR PLAN

FIRST-FLOOR PLAN

The house features ample outdoor rooms and facilities, including a shower by the beach (*above*), an expansive deck at the front of the house and terraces across both levels of the two-storey building.

The blue sofa at the far end of the living room is a bespoke piece by the architects (*left*); the swimming pool passes through the space just behind it. The two swivel armchairs are by Carlos Motta. In the entrance hallway (*above*), a suspended sculpture forms a dramatic focal point.

The master suite on the upper level
flows out onto an elevated private
terrace with an ocean view. A timber
pergola provides shade, while the glass
balcony means that the open view is
uninterrupted. The outdoor sofa is
a bespoke piece by the architects.

The terrace to the master bedroom (*above*) provides enough space for breakfast and dining outside. The central courtyard (*above right*) offers a more sheltered and private outdoor room with 'Asturias' armchairs by Carlos Motta. The veranda at the front of the house (*opposite*, *bottom right*) features an outdoor lounge with a barbecue and bar close at hand.

HOUSE FOR A PHOTOGRAPHER II

CARLOS FERRATER ALCANAR, CATALONIA, SPAIN

Photographer José Manuel Ferrater first got to know the Costa del Azahar as a child. He still cherishes fond memories of the prawns at the Can Pa Torrat restaurant in a small village down by the sea, not far from the town of Alcanar. This coastal enclave is now a second home and an alternative to his daily life in Barcelona.

For many years Ferrater had a cottage here, in the middle of an orange grove, but without a sea view. Then he came across a quiet site looking directly onto the gravel beach and the sea. It is one of a series of linear strips facing the water, with a number of the neighbouring gardens planted with vegetables and fruit trees. The atmosphere is calm and inviting, with a pair of concrete defence posts – relics from the Spanish Civil War – resting on the beach. The terrain, which forms part of the delta of the River Ebro, is flat and gentle, in contrast to the cliffs and promontories seen further north along the coastline.

Naturally, Ferrater turned to his brother, the much-respected Spanish architect Carlos Ferrater, to design the new house. The brief was a simple one, yet the resulting home is extraordinary and poetic. The architect designed three separate but complementary single-storey pavilions, positioned towards the back of the site, with smooth, rendered exteriors painted a crisp white. The pavilions sit on a floating timber platform, raised 70 cm (28 in.) off the ground, to protect against flooding, with the space between forming a sheltered outdoor terrace.

The dominant pavilion faces the sea and contains the main open-plan living area, with the furniture arranged around the view, visible through a large picture window. This pavilion also contains a kitchen island, and the high ceiling height allows a mezzanine ledge above the front window to be used as a display niche for sculpture and art.

Fifty-two mature palm trees, sourced locally, provide a graphic garden that sits between the house and the beach. The grove forms a vibrant hinterland, full of shadows and movement.

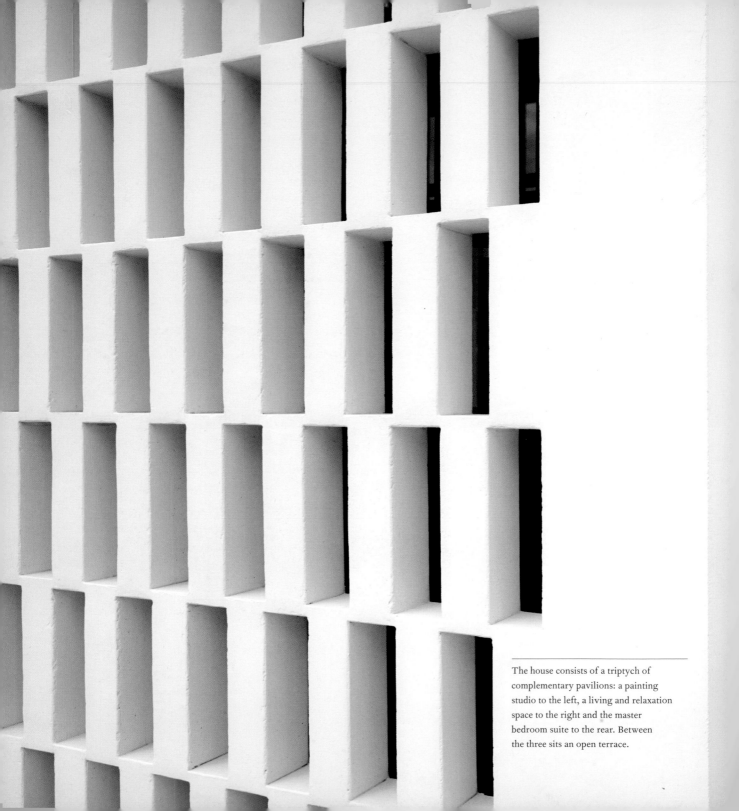

The house consists of a triptych of
complementary pavilions: a painting
studio to the left, a living and relaxation
space to the right and the master
bedroom suite to the rear. Between
the three sits an open terrace.

A secondary pavilion houses a painting studio, with a latticed brise soleil to filter the light; a small shower room and guest quarters are positioned to the rear, and an external staircase leads to a viewing platform on the roof. A third pavilion, pushed further back, holds the master bedroom and bathroom. The soaring ceilings suggest a sense of volume within a limited floor plan, while the generous roof height is fully utilized with the inclusion of a high-level library.

An original cottage of modest scale to the rear of the site was restored and a hydroponic vegetable garden created alongside it, sheltered by lemon and mulberry trees. In the front garden, the neat rows of Washingtonia palm trees, sourced from the same village and transplanted to site, echo the lines of planting in the neighbouring gardens, but on a grander scale. The tree trunks filter the view and offer a degree of privacy. The relationship between this house of three parts and the Mediterranean is a subtle one. The sea is a constant presence, but there is a sense of mediation between home, beach and water. The sound of the waves is soft but remains a constant, and is the dominant sound, along with the call of sea birds.

'At any time of the day and during any season of the year, you feel a sense of excitement with the experience of being here,' says Ferrater. 'I have three favourite spaces: the inside of the painting studio; underneath the mulberry and lemon trees when dining outside in summer; and in the living room at sunset with a glass of wine, sitting facing the window and the garden of palm trees and the sea.'

The main pavilion is an open-plan space with a kitchen island to the rear. Seating is arranged around a large window facing the palm grove and the sea; a mezzanine ledge forms a niche for the display of art and personal treasures, many of which were collected during travels in Africa and Asia.

The master suite is contained within a pavilion at the rear of the property. The high ceilings allow for an integrated library around the uppermost portion of the bedroom (*opposite and above left*). The lounge pavilion features a bespoke steel-faced kitchen island (*above*).

The palm grove creates a green blanket
that floats above the site and provides
shade and delight (*above*); the formation
of the trees echoes the planting of the
neighbouring gardens. The house itself
offers a crisp backdrop for the display of
art, curios and collected treasures (*opposite*).

OCEAN
BELVEDERE

OCEAN BELVEDERE

The idea of the genius loci – the unique spirit of a place – has particular relevance for the coast and the water's edge. The Romans saw the genius loci as a guardian spirit and guiding intelligence, to be revered with shrines as if it were a minor deity. Today we have taken the idea and given it new meaning, referring to the importance of context and setting for both architecture and landscape architecture.

With too much architecture and development having very little concern for context, genius loci has assumed particular resonance. Emphasis is placed on a sensitivity and responsiveness to the surroundings and choice of materials, suited to the area and climate, and lessons are there to be learnt from traditional dwellings and local building customs, although the references may be subtle and discreet when seen through the prism of contemporary design.

For waterside homes, the notion of genius loci has obvious importance. These are often houses built in places of environmental sensitivity, which demand special respect for their surroundings. There may well be a number of restrictions and planning conditions in place to limit the impact of any development. But just as important is an imaginative response and an essential understanding of the character of the landscape and forging of a close bond between the building and the natural beauty of the setting.

Architects Bates Masi took just such an approach when designing a house on the southern tip of Long Island (p. 108). The house itself is called 'Genius Loci', and there are references to traditional materials, although the approach is distinctly modern. More than this, the building responds to the vista of the water. Its prominent hillside position offers a prime vantage point for taking in views of the lake, the bay and the Atlantic beyond, and the house becomes a belvedere for appreciating these extraordinary vistas.

The belvedere – a building in an elevated location planned around a powerful view, with plenty in the way of glazing and open apertures – has long been a part of coastal living. Lighthouses and coastguard buildings have all used the idea of elevation to connect with the sea. The same is true of countless houses over the centuries that have sought to forge a close and meaningful relationship with the ocean by taking the high ground.

Many coastlines around the world do not offer easy access or sandy beaches, and yet the draw of the sea and the rugged beauty of the setting remains enticing

and engaging. The height offered by a clifftop or hillside creates a golden opportunity to design a home that offers a magical watchtower quality. These are houses that become platforms for appreciating the open water and its passing traffic, the changing weather patterns of sea and sky and the shifting seasons. The settings are often dramatic, and the genius loci strong and individual.

Architect Jordi Garcés and his client Nuria Amat collaborated on the design of a home perched upon the clifftops, near Tamariu on the Costa Brava (p. 116). Each of the key living spaces has floor-to-ceiling walls of glass overlooking the Mediterranean and feeding out onto elevated terraces. Further along the coast, the architectural team of Cadaval & Solà-Morales designed a house on the Cap de Creus that is essentially a series of lenses (p. 98), with each aperture focused on the rugged shoreline and sea in an area that is part of a natural coastal preserve.

In many instances, the main living spaces are positioned on the upper levels of the house to make the most of the best vantage points, as with Rob Mills's Ocean House in Lorne, Australia (p. 126), where the open-plan living areas and a roof terrace offer an open vista of the sea. The same is true

of Peter Stutchbury and Fergus Scott's Cliff Face House on the Pittwater peninsula, north of Sydney (p. 160).

Such houses are often intricately woven into the sloping topography of the site, stepping down the cliff and embracing the ocean view. This is very much the case with Iain Halliday's Whale Beach House, near Sydney (p. 168), and Duangrit Bunnag's house in Phuket, Thailand (p. 144), which respond to the genius loci by shaping the building in concert with the gradient and character of the coast.

Extreme conditions and situations require not only specialist engineering and careful construction, but also a particular attention to the choice of materials, which must be long-wearing and low maintenance, with a resistance to the salt air. For their clifftop project in Palos Verdes, California (p. 136), Marmol Radziner chose a palette of materials with great care, including a titanium roof, steel-framed windows and local stone, all able to withstand the salty spray.

Waterside houses must be designed with a respect not just for the sense of place, but also those occasional extremes and winter storms that occur along the coast. Turbulent weather, from a point of safety and sanctuary, can become a point of wonder when seen from a belvedere by the sea.

CAP D'ANTIBES HOUSE

KALLOSTURIN CAP D'ANTIBES, FRANCE

The French Mediterranean coast held a particular allure for the twentieth-century modernists. One thinks, in particular, of the crisp, white outline of Eileen Gray's E-1027 at Roquebrune-Cap-Martin, completed in 1929; Le Corbusier, who built a modest cabin nearby, described it as one of his favourite places. Here, on the Cap d'Antibes, the notion of the sleek modernist villa was a key inspiration when it came to transforming an unremarkable Provençal-style house into a contemporary home suited to twenty-first-century waterside living.

'The client was inspired by E-1027, as well as the early Le Corbusier villas,' says architect Stephania Kallos, 'so the main architectural elements pay homage to it: the flat roof, white stucco walls, floor-to-ceiling windows and the spiral stairs to the bedroom level. But the ocean was really the primary reference – you can see, smell and hear it from every room in the house.'

The clients are based in London for much of the year, but have formed a strong attachment to Antibes. When visiting friends on the Cap, they noticed that a neighbouring house was for sale and leapt at the opportunity to buy it. Noting an earlier KallosTurin-designed project in Provence, the family turned to the architects, requesting a radical reinvention of the existing building. To all intents and purposes, the resulting project is a new house.

Gently tucked into the sloping hillside, the building offers a powerful vantage point over the Mediterranean. The main living spaces are contained on the ground floor, which also includes the entrance, accessed via the freshly landscaped rear garden. Seating, dining and kitchen areas are arranged in an open plan, although a modest screen dating from the 1970s provides some separation between the kitchen

The crisp, white stucco of the exteriors stands out against the blue skies and open water. The design of the building makes the most of its elevated vantage point overlooking the sea.

and the rest of the main living zone. Floor-to-ceiling sliding glass windows frame the view and open onto a balcony and dining terrace, which look down to the new pool and terrace below.

This lower ground level was partially reclaimed from a former sunken garage and now holds three bedrooms and service spaces. Each of these bedrooms flows out to the pool terrace, which is partially shaded by the balcony above. The uppermost level is devoted to a large master suite, with a private balcony of its own, offering a welcome level of privacy and quiet isolation for the owners. There is also a partially sheltered terrace alongside and a roof terrace above, which is generally used in the early mornings or evening when the sun is lower in the sky.

The interiors are largely painted a soothing white, providing a neutral backdrop for the introduction of colour and texture through the furnishings. The furniture choices include a number of iconic mid-century pieces, such as Serge Mouille ceiling lights and chairs by Poul Kjærholm. Floors are in Florentine sandstone, with herringbone oak for the master bedroom. The bathroom is enlivened with the use of an earthy green mosaic around the shower enclosure and marble bathtub. Outside, an additional 'room' was created in the rear garden, surrounded by lush planting in the form of succulents, cacti and citrus trees to a design by Anthony Paul. Exterior furniture is by Paola Lenti.

'The clients find the house to be a quiet refuge,' says Kallos. 'Having the master suite at the top of the house with the guestrooms on the lower ground level means that they can have family and friends to stay, yet still feel this sense of privacy. And I love the fact that the ocean has such a strong presence in every space.'

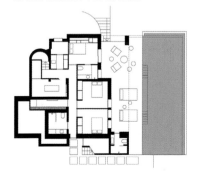

The three-storey house features a range of outdoor living spaces on every level, including the roof. The swimming pool terrace is populated with outdoor seating by Paola Lenti.

The living areas occupy one open-plan
space at mid-level. In front of a bespoke
fireplace made with Florentine sandstone
is a 'Unicorn' sofa by Vladimir Kagan
(*left*). The ceiling light in the dining room
is by Serge Mouille; the chairs are by
Gio Ponti and Carlo di Carli (*above*).

The wall and ceiling lights in the master bedroom, which is situated on the top floor of the house, are by Serge Mouille (*opposite*). Sculptural pieces, splashes of vibrant colour and the sea views make for a multi-layered home rich in character and interest (*above and left*).

OPORTI HOUSE

CADAVAL & SOLÀ-MORALES PORT DE LA SELVA, CATALONIA, SPAIN

The Cap de Creus peninsula has a very particular and individual kind of beauty. This part of the Costa Brava, not far from the French-Catalonian border, is a protected natural park and is unspoiled by the rampant development that has blighted other parts of the Spanish coastline. The area is popular with those who love the sea, good wine and seafood, as well as beloved by hikers and naturalists.

As they make their way along the coastal path, not far from the town of El Port de la Selva, some of these hikers stop and take note of a striking, contemporary house on a hillside overlooking the Mediterranean. The house, owned and commissioned by Geoff Roberts and Melinda Taylor as a year-round retreat from their daily working life in The Hague, is formed of ten intersecting cubes, which create a series of lenses facing the water and framing views of the sea and coastline.

'We wanted to frame each of the amazing scenes that the site offered,' says architect Eduardo Cadaval of the Barcelona-based practice Cadaval & Solà-Morales. 'So we came up with this idea of having not just one frontal view, but ten different ones.'

Both Roberts, who grew up in England, and Australian-born Taylor share a love of Spain, and particularly the coast. They began searching for a suitable site for a house that they could drive to, if needed, as well as flying; they were also attracted by the idea of being close to Barcelona, and narrowed their search to the Costa Brava. Taylor managed to find the site on an Internet hunt and spotted some work by Cadaval & Solà-Morales. When the couple contacted the architects, they were pleased to find that Clara Solà-Morales knew the Cap de Creus particularly well, given that her parents live in El Port de la Selva and she spent part of her childhood here.

The façade of the house offers a series of angled lenses framing views of the ocean. Large picture windows draw the vista inside the home; the coffee table is by Italian design company Kartell and the elephant stool by Charles and Ray Eames (*opposite*).

The couple and their two children asked for a retreat that made the most of the sea views, but was also practical and low maintenance. 'We wanted family and friends to be able to come and visit us, and needed different spaces to accommodate people in different areas of the house, but without creating lots of individual rooms that are shut away from one another,' says Roberts.

The house is pushed into the sloping site, with a terrace to the front and an infinity pool facing the sea. A secondary terrace is tucked away to the rear, creating a sheltered zone that offers protection from the occasional *tramontana* winds. The main living spaces and kitchen on the ground floor are largely open plan and arranged around a central double-height atrium. The projecting cubes help define more distinct areas for dining and sitting, as well as framing views of the sea, while a high rear window brings additional light into the atrium. Upstairs, two bedrooms are arranged to one side of the atrium with a further two accessed across a bridge that spans the central void.

This exceptional holiday home is used by the family all year round, including the winter. The white stucco render helps protect the house from the salt air, and reinforced glazing provides robust protection from the sea breezes, making the house a protective, endearing shell, suited to every season.

'Even in winter, because of the large glass windows and the diffusion of natural light, it feels as though you are sitting outside,' Roberts says. 'During windy gales or storms, it's stunning to watch the waves crashing on the rocks and the changing patterns in the sky and ocean, while being safely ensconced inside.'

GROUND-FLOOR PLAN

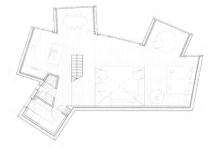

FIRST-FLOOR PLAN

The building consists of ten intersecting cubes, each capturing a slightly different vista. The steep approach was terraced to provide a swimming pool at one level and a series of terraces adjoining the house.

The main living area at the heart of the house is arranged around a double-height atrium (*left*), which draws in light from both levels of the house. Natural alcoves formed by the intersecting cubes form rooms within a room, as seen in the dining area with its dramatic sea view (*above*).

The light, sculptural staircase forms a
partial divider between the custom kitchen
and the rest of the open-plan living space
(*opposite and left*); the red stools are by
Magis. A suspended fireplace by Traforart
forms an anchor for the seating area with
its Italsofa couch (*top left*), while the
master bedroom benefits from one of
the best views of the Cap (*above*).

A slim walkway connecting the bedrooms crosses the double-height atrium on the upper level, with a vast picture window to one side and a glass balcony to the other (*opposite*). The swimming pool offers a visual splice with the ocean when viewed from the house or terrace (*above*).

GENIUS LOCI

BATES MASI ARCHITECTS LONG ISLAND, NEW YORK, USA

Clinging to the tip of the southern fork of Long Island, the town of
Montauk has a rugged, informal charm. This is literally the end of the
road, where the Montauk Highway meets the Atlantic, after passing
through the desirable, well-heeled communities of the Hamptons.
Montauk has a different character to its neighbours, and it was this
spirit – the 'genius loci' – that formed the key point of inspiration
and departure for a modern home designed by Bates Masi Architects.

Harry Bates and Paul Masi know this part of the world intimately
and have based their practice – and much of their work – in the area
for many years. Masi grew up in Montauk and still has a strong affection
for the place, so when it came to designing a new home up on a hillside
within a former horse ranch, the firm was well placed to formulate a
considered and sensitive response.

'We kept talking about a sense of place,' says Masi. 'There is this
very unexpected character to the area as a whole, and that was the
premise of the project: exploring the unique character that separates
Montauk from the Hamptons.'

This journey of exploration encompassed a number of different
aspects. Above all, there was a response to the site and its topography,
with the house pushed into the hillside. This helps reduce the outward
appearance of the building and its impact on the landscape, and placing
all the main living spaces and the family bedrooms on the upper level
means that the best of the views are both captured and enhanced. From
this elevated position the vista takes in the waters of Lake Montauk,
Gardiners Bay and the Atlantic Ocean.

Although the house is relatively large, the architects were keen to
further reduce the impact of the building by not only tucking it into

The swimming pool and pool terrace are set a
short but comfortable distance from the main
house, while a pool house is tucked away to one
side down a small flight of steps. The outdoor
furniture is by Paola Lenti.

the hillside, but also dividing the structure into two distinct parts connected by a bridge at the upper level. This lends the house a degree of modesty, with all the services, garaging, guestrooms and gym on the lower storey. An entry courtyard separates the two distinct elements of the building. There was also a particular approach in the use of materials, reinterpreting vernacular references within a contemporary aesthetic and a crisp outline. The pitched roof, too, echoes traditional buildings of the region, yet is given a literal and metaphorical twist.

'From a distance, the house looks like a bungalow,' says Masi. 'Then you come up closer and see that it is something more elaborate. That's a reflection of Montauk itself – at first it seems like everywhere else on Long Island, but as you get further into it, there's a lot of depth.'

The family can use the upper level as a self-contained home within a home, with the main living spaces, including the kitchen, sitting in an open-plan zone at one end of the building, bordered by terraces that dissolve the boundaries between inside and outside living. The bridge of glass, coated in tapered cedar boards that act as a brise soleil, contains a study, plus two elevated decks. Across the bridge are the children's bedrooms and the master suite, with private decks of their own.

A swimming pool and pool house are also perched on the hillside, but set slightly apart from the main building. From certain angles, the infinity pool seems to blur with the waters of Lake Montauk. Contextuality is everything here, as well as in the landscaping, which was achieved by using indigenous planting. The results are accomplished, subtle and satisfying, and a world away from some of the brash mansions further back along the coast.

GROUND-FLOOR PLAN

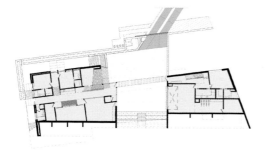

FIRST-FLOOR PLAN

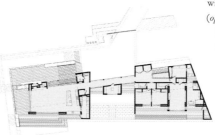

The surface of the infinity pool merges with the bay, with the ocean in the distance (*opposite*). The two-storey house is divided into two parts, connected by an enclosed bridge, which also holds a study (*above*).

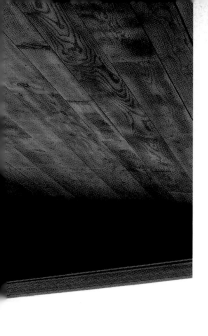

The main living spaces are on the upper level and are open plan, with glazed walls that slide back to offer a free-flowing relationship with the adjoining terraces. The sofa is from De La Espada, and the two armchairs are by BassamFellows.

The hallway and stairwell on the lower
level offer glimpses of the outside and
are enhanced by a rich quality of light
(*opposite and above left*); a fitted banquette
offers a conversation point and a place
for changing shoes. Natural light and a
strong indoor-outdoor relationship are
promoted throughout, with the master
bedroom and bathroom (*left and above*)
leading out to a private terrace.

SILVER HOUSE

JORDI GARCÉS TAMARIU, GIRONA, SPAIN

The Costa Brava has many delights. Tucked away between the larger towns and ribbons of coastal sprawl are hidden bays and small communities, where charm and character still prevail. One of these gems is Tamariu, a small seaside town, where fishing boats are still drawn up on the beach. It's no wonder that the client, Catalan novelist and poet Nuria Amat, was drawn to Tamariu even as a child, and has been making her way back here from her native Barcelona ever since.

'I have always dreamed of having a house by the sea, on the Costa Brava,' says Amat. 'When I would come and stay in Tamariu I would ask if anyone knew of any land for sale, and then about ten years ago I found a place to build a house. I liked the view of the sea, the trees and the landscape, and the house itself is like a boat caught on the rocks.'

Amat turned to architect Jordi Garcés to design a contemporary building on the edge of the town. The position is a dramatic one, perched high upon the sandstone cliffs overlooking the Mediterranean. Architect and client wanted to preserve the character of the site and created a design that works around the steep slope of the hillside, with a series of intersecting boxes accommodating four separate floor levels.

From the street access to the rear you step into the uppermost level of the house, which holds a gallery containing a guest suite and a study area. Yet the main living area and principal entrance are situated on the main floor level below, which holds the kitchen, dining area and a large sitting room in an L-shaped, open-plan formation. The windows are carefully positioned here to maximize views of the sea and to avoid connecting with the sightlines of the neighbouring houses. Sliding glazing also opens up to an adjoining dining terrace, partially sheltered by the rocks and the body of the house itself.

The house is slotted into the rocky terrain, with an infinity pool looking out across the water at the uppermost portion of the site. Steps lead down to the main entrance and the key living areas of the house; additional terraces are positioned lower down the cliff.

The way the multi-level building clamps itself to the steep cliff is best appreciated when viewed from the pool terrace. The main living spaces are contained within one of the upper levels, with the majority of the bedrooms positioned lower down the cascading house.

The private nature of the house is preserved on the lower levels, which hold a further three bedrooms, all with a strong relationship with the ocean. This is particularly true of the master suite, with a panoramic view of the sea from the floor-to-ceiling windows. The red sandstone pushes into the house, with an exposed wall of rugged stone forming a backdrop to a sculpted bathtub, which sits to one side of the bedroom.

The master suite leads out onto a private terrace overlooking the water; it is one of a series of tiered terraces and gardens, while an infinity pool is positioned on the uppermost portion of the site. A series of steps were also cut into the steep cliffside, which wind down to the sea and provide access to a private bathing area. From here, the true drama of the cliffs can be appreciated, along with the ingenuity contained within the process of designing and building a house in such an exposed but powerful position.

Amat designed the interiors herself, adopting a silver theme that was in keeping with the modernity of the house. The rendered surface of the exterior walls were painted a shimmering silver colour, and a number of bespoke items of furniture by Garcés pick up on the metallic theme. The colour sits in stark but engaging contrast to the organic quality of the surrounding rocks. The great achievement of the house is not to stand out – like some of its neighbours – but to adapt to the topography of the cliffs. For the architect, the subtle relationship of the building to the site is one of the most successful aspects of the project.

'The Silver House is an ideal place to do anything you like,' says Amat. 'In my case, that is writing and living, open to the sea. I like the originality of the house above everything.'

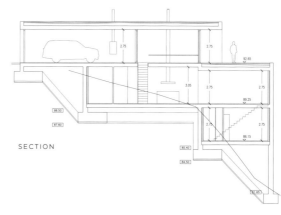

SECTION

The main living spaces are all contained on one level in an L-shaped formation, including the sitting area, dining zone and kitchen, with the outdoor dining terrace close by. The dining table is by Eero Saarinen and the dining chairs are by Arper; the sofas are from Living Divani.

The master bedroom (*opposite and above left*) features a bathtub with a dramatic backdrop of exposed rock. A dining terrace (*top left*) has been tucked among the rocks alongside the main living spaces, with easy access to the kitchen (*above*).

The infinity pool and terrace sit at the top of the site, with dramatic views of the coastline (*left*). The rendered walls of the house have been painted a reflective silver (*above*), which helps to repel the heat of the summer sun and keep the house cool, along with natural cross-ventilation.

OCEAN HOUSE

ROBERT MILLS LORNE, VICTORIA, AUSTRALIA

Architect Robert Mills is a creature of habit. He has been coming down to the seaside town of Lorne, a few hours' drive from Melbourne, for the past nineteen years. For many summers he rented a house here, but when he saw that a piece of land had come up for sale on the very same street, he seized the opportunity and began to think about designing a new house for himself, his partner and his two daughters.

'It has been an ambition to build my own beach house,' says Mills, whose practice is based in Melbourne. 'As an architect, building your own home is when you really get to express yourself and test your ideas. When you are working for a client, your primary role is to make their dreams and aspirations come alive, but you don't necessarily get to explore your own ambitions and whims. So when you do get a chance to build for yourself, it's a real opportunity.'

For some time after buying his parcel of land overlooking Loutit Bay, Mills intended to build a timber cabin. But a tightening up of planning conditions for timber homes in the wake of a series of bush fires led to a more ambitious design for a three-storey house, made principally of concrete. This new home would have a family space on the top floor, with four self-contained bedrooms and living spaces on the floors below, which could be rented out to help subsidize the running costs.

The house is pushed into a steep hillside and runs almost parallel to the sea, capturing the best of the views. Mills's personal realm on the top floor has a fresh, fluid feel with an open-plan kitchen, dining area and sitting room placed within a pavilion and banks of timber-framed glass connecting to the seascape. There is also an elevated terrace alongside, complete with an outdoor table, as well as a breakfast bar alongside the kitchen, where a window retracts to form a serving hatch.

As well as a series of balconies and terraces, the house also features a rooftop deck complete with a fire pit; this makes for a perfect spot for evening entertaining with a view, as well as a daytime sanctuary.

The floors throughout are in polished concrete with underfloor heating; natural cross-ventilation cools the house in summer. Ceilings and bespoke kitchen cabinets made from blackbutt, a native hardwood, lend a more organic flavour, helped by the verdant greenery and tree canopy that borders the building.

'The house needed to be at one with the forest and the sea,' says Mills. 'The colours are calming, and I love to live with the colour grey. The timber is naturally a light-brown colour, but has a hint of grey in it. We put a chalky wash over it, then rubbed it down a little and left the chalk in the grain, so that it works well with the concrete.'

The curving walls of a stucco drum at the far end of the pavilion, holding the fireplace and log store, suggest a change of direction at the opposite end of the house, where the sinuous shapes recall a ship's hull. The master bedroom is circular, and the Patricia Urquiola-designed bed sits within a relaxing space bordered with linen curtains, which hide the bath, shower and other elements contained in an outer circle. Other bedrooms are woven around this circular room, while up on the roof the rounded forms are echoed by a roof terrace, complete with a fire pit and day beds. Mills tends to come up here in the evenings and late afternoon, as it's a spot that captures an extra hour or two of sunshine before the sun sinks behind the nearby hillside.

The character of the house is elegant but also casual, informal and relaxed. On Mondays the dining table becomes a drawing board, where Mills works before heading back to his office in the city. And unlike many devotees of Lorne – which turns sleepy and quiet out of season – Mills now comes out here all year round.

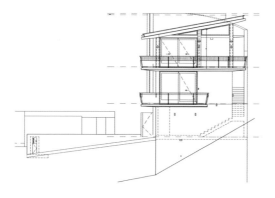

ELEVATION

The main living spaces on the upper level – including the kitchen – open out onto a partially sheltered terrace with sun loungers, a dining table and a fresh-air breakfast bar (*opposite*).

The multi-level building is pushed into the gradient of the slope and positioned parallel to the beach and the ocean, creating a long run of spaces with an open view of the water.

The main living spaces are on the top floor to make the most of the views and the light (*above*); the circular coffee tables are an Eero Saarinen design from Knoll and the sofa is from Living Divani. The kitchen is also custom-designed and made; the pendant light is by Gubi (*opposite*).

The dining table is a bespoke piece designed by Robert Mills (*opposite*), made with blackbutt timber; the dining chairs are by Eero Saarinen. The black armchairs at the other end of the room are from Hub (*above*). The master bedroom (*above left and left*) offers glimpses of the ocean via a wraparound curtain, which also lends privacy to the integrated bath.

ALTAMIRA RESIDENCE

MARMOL RADZINER PALOS VERDES, CALIFORNIA, USA

The Altamira Residence manages to accommodate two very different ambitions. Situated upon a clifftop site on the Palos Verdes peninsula, the house needed to maximize the views of the ocean, the coastline and Catalina Island. At the same time, the clients and their architects shared a desire to create a building of some subtlety and sensitivity, which would not overwhelm the natural beauty of the site, but would work with the existing topography and character of the setting.

The design solution achieves this in a number of ways. Firstly, rather than create one large dwelling, the programme was broken down into a number of smaller parts within a compound formation. These include a guest house, a study and a subterranean garage, as well as the main residence. Secondly, these buildings are arranged around the natural gradient of the site, as it slopes down gently towards a steep cliff, which then falls away to the beach below. Tucking the house into the landscape mitigates the visual impact of the building and helps preserve the ocean vista for neighbouring residents.

'We also stretched the house, so we could pick up the views directly out towards Catalina, as well as to the north, along the coast,' says architect Ron Radziner. 'There is a view straight out to the ocean, but that sideways view is also very beautiful and takes advantage of the pieces of land jutting out into the sea further up the coastline.'

The client first approached the firm after meeting during the design and build of a school in the region, which he had contributed towards. The client and his family had recently acquired an 8-hectare (20-acre) parcel of land, adjacent to their former home on the Palos Verdes peninsula, an area rich in natural beauty that lies to the west of Long Beach and south of Los Angeles.

The house makes the most of its elevated position; the design optimizes views of the sea and the coastline, with its rugged promontories.

'It is very unusual to have such a large parcel of land here,' says Radziner. 'Most of the homes here are much closer together. But there were also many other factors we had to consider. It is a rugged cliff and very steep, so you can't just walk down to the beach – you have to circle round to get down to the sea. As it can be a little bit windy along the coast, we needed to create areas where the family could be outside, but have some protection from the wind coming off the ocean.'

A substantial outdoor room was created around the pool terrace at the front of the house, complete with a fireplace. This fresh-air entertaining space is partially sheltered by projecting walls of shale stone, quarried from the site, while an outdoor kitchen is tucked away to one side. A series of lightly interconnected living spaces push outwards from the front of the building and make the most of the views. Service spaces and bedrooms for the children are sited towards the rear.

The upper level is devoted solely to the master suite: a private and self-contained retreat with a bedroom and bathroom, walk-in closet, study and two decks, as well as a balcony. The interiors feature bespoke and integrated elements throughout, from the custom kitchen to the bespoke dining table. Exterior materials were chosen for their texture and colour (a soothing palette of greys), and durability in the sea air. Window frames are in painted steel and the roof is titanium, creating a robust, hard-wearing combination that requires little maintenance.

'The house integrates into the site pretty well,' says Radziner. 'It sits low and tight to the landscape. I like the fact that for a big home it breaks up into all these different components and works harmoniously with its surroundings.'

GROUND-FLOOR PLAN

FIRST-FLOOR PLAN

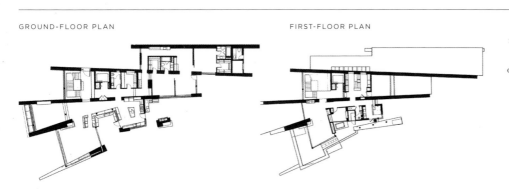

The indoor-outdoor relationship is maximized with sliding glass walls in the key living spaces (*above*), and a series of outdoor rooms arranged around the pool and other parts of the house (*opposite*).

The main living spaces feature bespoke elements such as the dining table (*opposite*) and the kitchen (*above left*), designed by the architects and made from walnut. The dining room, living room (*above*) and kitchen form a sequence of interconnected spaces with views of the ocean.

The upper level of the house is devoted to the master suite, which includes a private study and dressing room, as well as the master bathroom and adjoining decks with open views of the Pacific; there is space on one of the decks for an integrated hot tub.

EV06 HOUSE

DUANGRIT BUNNAG PHUKET, THAILAND

There are few parts of Asia quite as seductive as the island of Phuket. Here, on the coast overlooking the picture-perfect Phang Nga Bay, Anthony and Anna Wilkinson have created an enticing new home for themselves and their family. It is a house that frames an engaging view of the bay: a Marine National Park, rich in natural diversity and birdlife. Such is the calm, natural beauty of the location that the couple have christened the house 'Serenity'.

Having found the site, perched upon a sloping cliff with views over the water, the couple were introduced to architect Duangrit Bunnag. For Bunnag, who also designed the Naka Phuket hotel on the island and knows the area well, the site itself represented an irresistible opportunity. 'This side of Phuket is unique,' he says. 'It is an architect's dream to build on a site like this – on a slope overlooking the ocean, with this cascading topography.'

As the clients wanted privacy and a contemporary design, as well as light, air and a strong relationship with the surroundings, Bunnag's design turns its back on the access road and explores the connection to the ocean as fully as possible, with a building that steps down the cliff and embraces the vista. Entering the house from the rear, one has little sense of what to expect when stepping onto an entrance bridge over a lily pond and through a large timber doorway, set into a wall of grey stone. As you step onto another bridge overlooking a 'valley', or sunken courtyard, the house reveals itself further.

'The house looks quite normal from the outside and is very private,' says Bunnag, 'so as you emerge in this valley with a sunken fountain to one side and a waterfall to the other, it's a surprise. Because the building is finished with stone and other hard surfaces, we needed some balance,

The house is sensitively orientated around views of Phang Nga Bay, with the pool and terraces facing the water (*opposite*). A courtyard to the rear offers a more enclosed garden with planting and water pools (*below*).

Lush greenery and mature trees border the house, enhancing the feeling of privacy and promoting the sense of connection with nature, as well as with the bay itself.

so we put in trees and water features. But with the waterfall in the courtyard, what I was thinking about was sound as much as anything. When you walk into the house the sound of the water is very inviting.'

Beyond the courtyard, the upper level of the house is devoted to the main living spaces, with a generously scaled sitting room to one side leading into a combined dining room and kitchen. Both spaces have floor-to-ceiling windows looking out across the water, while the sitting room is complemented by an adjoining veranda tucked into the outline of the building.

The lower storey holds a study, family room, the master suite and two further bedrooms; another guestroom sits within a partial sub-level. Water pools provide a soothing backdrop to one side of the master bedroom; to the other is a view of the bay. A terraced deck and infinity-style swimming pool form a long plateau at the front of the house, with transparent glass balconies providing a barrier to the terraced cliffscape below. Glass has also been used to border the infinity pool, allowing the water and the ocean beyond to dissolve into one another.

'We used the kind of glass you would find in an aquarium,' says Bunnag. 'It gives the effect of continuity, and when you are swimming at the edge of the pool, you feel as though you are swimming into the ocean. It's a wonderful experience.'

This sense of connection with the bay remains constant throughout the building, with the lush greenery that surrounds the house forming a perfect foil to the crisp, geometrical composition. 'Serenity' is an appropriate name for a house with such a calm and escapist quality to it.

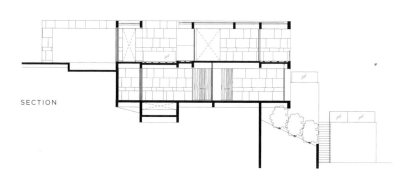

SECTION

The main living spaces have panoramic views of the sea, with walls of glass that slide back for an uninterrupted vista. The dining room and kitchen share one open space (*this page*), with the main living room alongside (*opposite*).

Layers of slate were used to provide
a backdrop to the waterfall in the
courtyard; the sound of water is a
constant presence in the house (*above*).
The sunken courtyard and fish pond
also help introduce natural light to
the lower storey of the house. Timber
floors and finishes add an organic
quality and create a sense of warmth
in the bedrooms and bathrooms (*above
left*) on the lower storey.

WATERFRONT HOUSE

JPR ARCHITECTS COOGEE BEACH, SYDNEY, AUSTRALIA

With its warm, organic character and a vivid relationship with the ocean, Waterfront House has its roots far away in a small fishing village in South Africa. The houses of Paternoster, on the Western Cape, are distinctive and engaging: softly rendered homes with rounded edges, arranged around the bay. The village made a lasting impression on a couple who wanted to commission a new house on a prime site, which offers a sublime waterside vista and easy access to downtown Sydney.

Fortuitously, architect Dennis Rabinowitz was already familiar with Paternoster. Like his clients, he is originally from South Africa and was all in favour of a house that spliced natural materials and rounded forms with a sensitive, contextual approach to the site. Other reference points included the adobe houses of New Mexico and the vernacular traditions of Bali and other parts of Asia – homes that combine traditional influences, natural materials and contemporary living.

'It's handcrafted architecture, rather than a manufactured building,' says Rabinowitz. 'It's very textured and organic. The walls of the house were consciously made to feel thick and robust, as this kind of architecture is earth-bound and grounded. The cement render is applied as though it were hand-packed mud, so you get that undulating finish.'

The clients, who have two daughters, got to know and understand Coogee Beach very well, having lived in another house alongside the site for a number of years. Their brief was highly detailed and carefully thought through, embodying design references along with a considered appraisal of how they wanted to live in the new house, as well as an appreciation of the climatic conditions of the site, including the occasional winds that sweep along the coast and the corrosive effect of the salt spray.

The rounded edges and timber pergolas soften the outline of the house, while the landscaping helps tie the building into its setting; the rounded boulders around the steps were brought in from the Snowy Mountains.

Two earlier buildings were removed to create room for the new house, pool and garden, which were designed around the views. The architecture also had to respond to the steep slope of the site, which drops away towards the sea, and the need to avoid overlapping sightlines with the neighbours. At the same time, the clients did not want a house on too many different levels.

To avoid this, the house is spread across the double-plot, offering what Rabinowitz describes as two interconnected 'bungalows', one on top of the other. The upper level provides the main entry route from the street via a sunken courtyard, which also provides a sheltered relaxation zone. The upper level has two bedrooms for the children, plus a master suite facing the sea, with a private balcony and a bathroom that balances privacy with glimpses of the ocean via a timber lattice brise soleil.

The main living spaces are located on the floor below and include an open-plan kitchen and dining area, with a separate living room alongside, all leading out to a veranda and decks arranged around an infinity pool. The relationship between indoor and outdoor space is fluid and easy, and the ocean is a constant presence. Carefully chosen materials include a range of native timbers of different textures and patinas, used for floors, ceilings and to support trellises and canopies.

'What really pleases us about the house is the simple, honest detailing and the magical places it offers,' says the client. 'The outside veranda off the kitchen is our favourite spot – it has northeast views, which are always terrific, and a wood fireplace we use every night in winter. Even in winter we have whales, clear, flat sea days and sunshine, and the full moons over the sea are just incredible.'

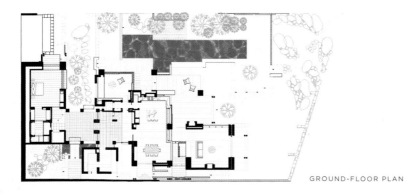

The poolside veranda (*opposite*) offers a secondary living room with an easy connection to the pool area and the ocean view; this sheltered space includes a fireplace and seating from Robert Plumb.

The living room is at the front of the house facing the ocean (*right*), with easy access to the pergola alongside, complete with a Nanna Ditzel-designed rattan chair; the sofa is from Cassina and the round table is from Mark Tuckey. The kitchen (*above*) is a bespoke design by the architect.

The house features many integrated pieces of furniture, including fitted seating and window seats (*above and right*), as well as integrated shelving in a bedroom on the upper storey (*opposite*). As with so many other parts of the house, the master bathroom uses a number of different timbers to reinforce the crafted, organic quality of the interiors (*above right*).

CLIFF FACE HOUSE

PETER STUTCHBURY / FERGUS SCOTT PALM BEACH, SYDNEY, AUSTRALIA

The Pittwater peninsula, north of Sydney, is a seductive setting. Its western edge faces an estuary marking the point where the Hawkesbury River feeds into the Pacific, and much of the land here is contained within the borders of the Ku-ring-gai Chase National Park. Cliff Face House, the result of a collaboration between architects Peter Stutchbury and Fergus Scott, looks westwards over these tidal waters, avoiding the more extreme conditions of exposed seaward spots.

The building, in deference to the beauty of its surroundings, is discreet and thoughtful. While many of the neighbouring houses aim for height and prominent vantage points, it is tucked below the level of the nearby street and steps down a steep sandstone cliff, which becomes an intrinsic part of the building. The house represented a welcome opportunity for a fresh collaboration between former colleagues (Scott was also taught by Stutchbury at university), supported by clients with an understanding of the commissioning and design process and a desire to create something unique, both to them and to the site.

As the clients' four grown-up sons have families of their own, the three-storey house, constructed with a framework of recycled blackbutt timber, needed to be adaptable to suit the needs of a couple living on their own, as well as the extended family. The design places all of the main living spaces, including the master suite, on the uppermost level. A generously scaled open-plan living area sits at the centre, with the master bedroom at one end and a veranda at the other, sheltered by a lantern-like, translucent polycarbonate roof.

'The upper level can be used as an almost self-contained space,' says Scott. 'The design was also determined by managing the outlook and the sun, which is why we articulated the roof to enable the qualities

The house sits upon a bluff looking out over the Hawkesbury River estuary. The building is discreetly tucked into the sandstone cliffs, but still makes the most of the waterside vista.

of the afternoon light to permeate the space, but also control it with operable sunscreens. But because it is a more protected site, we were able to present this lantern roof, which does have a delicacy to it.'

The roof also adds to the transparency of this part of the house, with the eye able to pass through the building from the courtyard at the back of the house to the sea in front of it when the house is at its most open, with sliding doors and sun screens pulled back. The courtyard, which includes a swimming pool, functions as a large outdoor room that complements the main living spaces and includes an outdoor kitchen and shower area.

The lower two levels cling, limpet-like, to the cliff. The exposed cliff face forms the rear wall to certain spaces on these lower storeys, while the thermal mass of the sandstone and strategically placed voids between the building and the cliff help to cool the house during the summer months. Two guestrooms, utility spaces and a study are positioned at mid-level, with a third guestroom and family room on the ground floor. Each of the three storeys is essentially just one room deep, owing to the constrained nature of the site, but the balconies and walkways at the front of the house offer additional circulation routes, as well as a framework for sliding panels that form a brise soleil.

It is an ingenious plan for a difficult and extraordinary site. The design manages to achieve an immediate engagement with the water and the surroundings. But with the building tucked into the cliff, it also allows passers-by and neighbours to see over the top of it, without interrupting the view. Few houses could be said to be so considerate and so sensitive, both to the landscape and to the needs of others.

SOUTH ELEVATION

WEST ELEVATION

The upper level contains the principal living spaces, courtyard and sheltered deck; the stairway steps down to the two lower levels holding bedrooms, bathrooms and a family room, all with ocean views.

The living spaces are arranged in an open-plan formation and make the most of the elevated vantage point and natural light, which is enhanced by a roof of translucent polycarbonate, supported by a lattice of timber beams; a balcony with integrated sunscreens runs the length of the façade.

Both the mid- and upper storeys of the house feature integrated balconies overlooking the water (*above*). The ground level (*above right and opposite*), which features a bedroom, bathroom and family room, also flows out onto adjoining terraces; here, the exposed rock of the cliff becomes a feature, both inside and out.

WHALE BEACH HOUSE

BURLEY KATON HALLIDAY WHALE BEACH, SYDNEY, AUSTRALIA

There is a distinctive Asian influence that pervades the architecture and design of this clifftop home at Whale Beach, to the north of Sydney. The house was commissioned by a family who spend part of their year living in Asia and commute back regularly to their native Australia. While living overseas, they noted the work of a number of architects, including the Japanese master Tadao Ando, renowned for his inventive and innovative use of concrete. It was an important point of reference that fed into the design brief put to architect Iain Halliday for a new house on the Northern Beaches, overlooking the ocean.

'We did take the simplicity of line and strict palettes of Japanese architects such as Ando as inspirations,' says Halliday. 'The extensive use of concrete is a direct reference. The clients also wanted a timeless and durable residence that didn't need repainting every year, with clearly defined areas for adults, guests and children, generous living areas and continuous outdoor spaces.'

The other key influence on the design was, of course, the dramatic topography and character of the site. Halliday knows the area intimately, having also designed the neighbouring house, as well as a residence for himself further along the coast. It's a steep site, leading down to the water below, with strong views of the open sea eastwards and the rugged, winding coastline, with the Careel Headland Reserve in one direction and Barrenjoey Lighthouse at the very tip of the peninsula in the other. Halliday also had to work around some of the groundworks and foundations that remained from an earlier building.

'The site is extremely steep and the planning controls ask for a stepping silhouette, which we translated into a series of individual boxes, each with a defined function,' says Halliday, who has known the

The house consists of a series of distinct 'boxes' that step down the steep site and face the sea. The swimming pool can be seen as one of these linear, geometric units.

clients for many years. 'The proximity to the water is what really makes it a special place to live, with the sound of the waves on the rocks below and the inescapable presence of the changing sky and water.'

The house consists of a series of four distinct levels, stepping down the slope and all facing the sea. The uppermost level holds the garage, entrance lobby and storage and utility spaces, with the master suite, guest suites and lobby on the floor below. The main living zone follows, holding an open-plan space overlooking the ocean that includes seating and dining areas, as well as the kitchen. A wall of floor-to-ceiling retractable glass frames the open vista, while also sliding back to provide an easy flow through to a sheltered, balconied terrace. The bottom level is devoted to bedrooms for the owners' two teenage children, as well as a family rumpus room and media space. It also feeds out onto the pool terrace and the swimming pool, which looks out to sea and over the tiered garden as its steps down to the rocks below.

The architects also designed the interiors, which include a mix of contemporary furniture by Minotti and others, along with mid-century classics by Hans J. Wegner, Poul Kjærholm and Eero Saarinen. The relationship between the interiors and outside living space is crucial throughout the house. The master suite flows out onto a private terrace and a gravel garden beyond, which sits on the projecting roof of the building below, while a glass balcony allows for an uninterrupted view.

'The owners like the sense of calm, order and the connection to the site,' Halliday says. 'It is a place that still feels fresh each time you arrive. It's elegant and a real contrast to some of the "look at me" houses that have recently been built in the area.'

ELEVATION

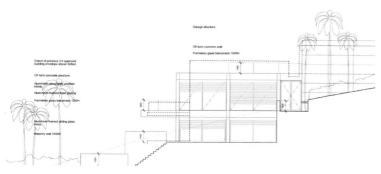

The interiors feature framed views of the sea and a number of indoor-outdoor spaces, including the pool terrace. A see-through glass balcony protects the pool without interrupting the view.

The main living area is at mid-level and
holds a seating area, dining zone and
kitchen, while sliding windows retract
to allow free flow to a generously scaled
balcony. The sofa is from Minotti and the
two 'PK22' chairs are by Poul Kjærholm.

The master suite (*above and opposite*) sits above the main living spaces, and enjoys an open view of the ocean and easy access to an integrated balcony; the chair and ottoman are by Charles and Ray Eames. In the kitchen, a marble counter contrasts with the concrete side wall (*right*).

CRESCENT HOUSE

WALLACE E. CUNNINGHAM ENCINITAS, CALIFORNIA, USA

The sculptural form of Wallace E. Cunningham's Crescent House was driven partly by the site and partly by the moon. It was lunar inspiration that guided the form of the crescent-shaped swimming pool, terrace and winding ramp that greets you when you first enter the building. It is a purposefully processional entrance process, heightening the sense of expectation and drama as you ascend the ramp to the terrace and the main living spaces on the top floor, which are contained within a more linear portion of the house facing the ocean view.

The open courtyard that gives the house its name serves many functions. It is a partially protected outdoor room, providing a fresh-air retreat away from the strong breezes that can affect this exposed part of the coastline between San Diego and Los Angeles. The pool also benefits from the warmth and protection that the courtyard provides. At the same time, there is a theatrical quality to the space, reminiscent of a stage with a framed view out to the ocean via a significant gap in the main body of the house, which passes over it like a bridge. This void offers a path through to the terraces at the front, which face the sea.

'The owners purchased the site for the view,' says Cunningham. 'What makes the location special is unquestionably its height above the ocean and panoramic width, with the vista of all of the environmental and atmospheric happenings that come with the ocean and sky.'

The client lived in San Diego before moving to Encinitas, and had been involved as a developer in the reinvention of a number of old and abandoned buildings in the city. He and his wife wanted to build a contemporary home for themselves and their extended family that would make the most of the clifftop site and accommodate both friends and their collections of art and books.

All of the main living spaces and the master suite are positioned on the upper level of the house and enjoy open vistas of the ocean; integrated balconies provide viewing platforms and outdoor rooms.

The topography of the land and the way the site rises gently towards the edge of the bluff meant that height would be needed to make the most of the ocean view. The solution was to invert the house, placing the main living spaces at the top of the building, while creating more sheltered outdoor areas to provide inviting alternatives to the ocean-facing terraces when the wind was blowing.

Garaging and services are tucked away at basement level, from which a curving ramp ascends to the terrace storey, which also houses guestrooms and ancillary spaces in the wings to either side. The true character of the house only reveals itself upon ascending once again, continuing the journey via the ramp or an internal staircase, which resembles the backbone and vertebrae of some vast animal.

The top floor spans the width of the site and has the best of the views, looking out over the water in one direction and onto the crescent terrace in the other. An open-plan living and dining area sits at the centre, with fluid connections through floor-to-ceiling glazing to elevated balconies. The kitchen is partially open to the dining area, with a separate pantry and media room beyond. The other wing of the house contains the master suite, with a private balcony facing the open sea.

This is a house of great drama, with a monumental quality resulting from the combination of sculpted lines and the use of exposed concrete and stone. The complex geometries and the intricate ceiling on the top floor, with its coffered skylights, recall the work of mid-century Californian master John Lautner. Yet this is a highly contextual building that is a very specific response to a unique and engaging site, with that added inspiration drawn from the moon.

GROUND-FLOOR PLAN

FIRST-FLOOR PLAN

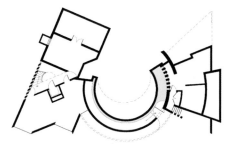

The enclosed courtyard provides a sheltered space bordered by a walkway (*opposite*); the outdoor furniture is from Brown Jordan. The dining area (*above*) is next to a seating zone and the kitchen.

The main seating area is anchored partly by the views of the ocean and partly by a triangular fireplace, which forms a key focal point. The sofa is from B&B Italia and the chairs are from Cassina, while the rug is a bespoke piece made by Savnik.

The angular architecture of the floor plan is reflected within the interiors, which feature many bespoke elements, including the fireplace in the sitting area, the custom kitchen and the angular dining table by Pamela Smith. The internal staircase (*opposite, top right*) is a feature piece by the architect, made from stainless steel. The picture in the master bedroom (*opposite, bottom left and right*) is by Manny Farber and the bed is by Piero Lissoni.

WATERFRONT VILLA

INTRODUCTION

'We need the tonic of wildness,' Henry David Thoreau wrote in *Walden*, published in 1854. 'At the same time that we are earnest to explore and learn all things, we require that things be mysterious and unexplorable, that land and sea be indefinitely wild, unsurveyed and unfathomed by us because unfathomable. We can never have enough of nature.'

Thoreau suggested, brilliantly, the ambiguity of our relationship with the natural world. We want to tame it on the one hand and to understand it, yet on the other we yearn for wild and undiscovered places. We want our own unspoilt landscapes and to have them, in one way or another, belong to us. This is particularly true of the coast and the waterside, which always arouse strong emotions and heartfelt reactions. The shore will always represent one of our most engaging and sacred places; we all have a favourite beach or a riverside walk. We want this to remain special and unique to us, even as it fills up with all those other people who might feel just the same way.

Building a house by the water is, in effect, a compromise of sorts. We make a home here because we are in love with the landscape and want to be able to appreciate it and enjoy it all the more. Yet we know that through the very act of

building, we are adding to the human footprint and making it a little more likely that future neighbours will want to come and do the same. It's a compromise that brings us back to the themes of modesty and sensitivity, to architect Glen Murcutt's idea of 'touching the earth lightly'. If we build a home, then let it be part of a considered and thoughtful process that seeks to lessen the impact upon the surroundings that delight us.

The beauty of waterside living is not, of course, only about the ocean. Lakes and waterways, river and estuaries share the natural power and beauty of the coast and are no less seductive, in their own ways. Even in a great city like London or Paris, living by, or having a view of, the river can transform your whole perception of the environment around you. Here is this flowing artery, with its own natural rhythm, that is also a ribbon of light and calm. To live by the river is to share in a sense of openness and peace, and to enjoy a very different perspective.

There is little wonder that the idea of living by the water attracts speculators and developers, eager to advertise a waterside view. In some parts of the world, the water itself becomes another place to live, offering an opportunity to

create floating homes and extend the inhabitable space of
a city, as we have seen in Amsterdam. In recent years, the
architecture and character of floating homes has improved
immeasurably, as architects and designers look to move
beyond traditional notions of a houseboat and seek a fresher
approach to the theme.

Among the more engaging reassessments of the floating
home stands Piet Boon's contemporary houseboat (p. 188).
As with so many new-generation floating homes, Boon's
two-storey project for a private client is not an adaptation or
conversion of a boat or pontoon, but rather a crafted modern
building that happens to float upon the water. It represents,
in a sense, a new typology, and is helped by the fact that it
also floats in a sublime setting at the side of a picturesque
Dutch lake, with open water to three sides and water reeds
and a green garden mooring to the other.

Other waterside homes that touch the earth lightly while
sitting on the shoreline seek to combine a discreet presence
with a strong sense of connection to the water and nature
itself. This is true of architect Seth Stein's Pencalenick
House (p. 208), in Cornwall, which sits on the edge of a
creek close to the mouth of the River Fowey. It is a large

residence, with seven bedrooms, yet by tucking it into
a sloping gradient surrounded by woodland, the house
becomes subtle and discreet.

The same is true of a riverside house in France designed
by Lode Architecture, on the banks of the River Odet, near
Quimper (p. 244). Architect and client agreed on a planting
strategy around the house, which enhances the layering of
trees, bushes and shrubs and creates a kind of green filter
between the building and the water. Passing boats and river
traffic are glimpsed through this natural curtain, while the
house itself almost disappears into the green camouflage
during the summer months. In the autumn, as the leaves
fall from the trees, the relationship with the river becomes
more open and direct, and a richer quality of light filtering
through the tree canopy helps compensate for the shorter
hours of daylight and the low sun.

In many ways these are homes that thrive upon the
'tonic of wildness'. They sit within sublime and spectacular
locations, while seeking to establish a true sense of
connection between interior and exterior worlds. They are
houses full of delight, which try to touch the earth lightly,
and never take the gift of waterside living for granted.

FLOATING HOME

PIET BOON AMSTERDAM, NETHERLANDS

When seen from the water, this crisp, geometric houseboat has an enigmatic quality. Coated in red cedar, which has been stained a dark organic colour, the floating box is mysterious in character and purpose when closed and resting. It is only as the integrated shutters are opened up that the house begins to unfold and reveal itself as a floating retreat, open to the water on three sides and partially sheltered and camouflaged by reed beds on the fourth.

The houseboat sits within a quiet spot on the edge of a lakeside harbour, to the south of Amsterdam, moored alongside a garden with a green backdrop of trees and reeds. The house was designed by Piet Boon (see also Kas Dorrie; p. 44) for returning clients, who had worked with the designer on two earlier house projects. The structure replaces an earlier houseboat on the site and the design approach challenges conventional thinking about the form and aesthetics of floating homes.

'When we design projects like this, we love to start from scratch and not be influenced by what is the norm,' says Boon. 'It is the best way to come up with unique and different solutions. The landscape is also a major point of consideration in every project, and we want our designs to blend in. That is why we decided on a subdued, silent and closed structure – a jewel box hiding its secrets.'

While moored in one static position, the houseboat needed the flexibility to move if needed and, of course, to reposition itself according to any fluctuations in the water level. Boon worked with a specialist builder to create a floating, water-tight, crafted shell. The programme required two floors of accommodation, but height restrictions meant that the building had to sit low against the mooring. The solution was a significant load of concrete ballast at the base of the

Water reeds form a protective green blanket around the house, providing a degree of privacy and softening the linear outline of the houseboat, which is coated in red cedar.

floating shell, ensuring that the houseboat sits low in the water. Two bedrooms with en-suite bathrooms sit within this lower storey, served by high slot windows just above the water line, which provide glimpses of the water world beyond and a welcome degree of natural light.

The open-plan living spaces of the upper level include the kitchen and an island, which doubles as a breakfast table, as well as a seating zone. Here, the protective cedar shutters and glazing fold away to allow a sense of open connection with the garden and introduce plenty of sunlight. A separate garden room sits at the far end of the houseboat: an indoor-outdoor space integrated into the outline of the building, where the shutters fold away to two sides, allowing for views of the lake.

Outside, a timber pergola sits on a wooden deck, creating an additional space for summer dining and entertaining. The family's boat is moored nearby, within a small cutting bordered by the water reeds. Furniture and furnishings inside and out mix bespoke designs and pieces from Boon's own furniture range. The lake and passing boats form a constant and enticing backdrop to daily life here. This is a house that is intimately connected to the rhythms of the water and the beauty of its natural surroundings. At the same time, its sensitivity to the setting creates a fresh and sophisticated way of thinking about contemporary floating homes. Rather than adapting a boat into a home, the approach has been to create a crafted home that also happens to float on the water.

'For us, it is the ultimate summer house,' says the client. 'The houseboat is compact but equipped with all the things that one could wish for. It blends in perfectly with the landscape, a fact that is much appreciated and acknowledged by our neighbours and the local people.'

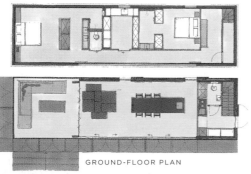

Protective shutters secure the houseboat when not in use (*above*), while a pergola forms a partially sheltered and shaded outdoor dining room (*opposite*).

A garden room – or integrated veranda
– is contained within the outline of the
rectangular timber building. This indoor-
outdoor sitting room has timber shutters
that can be open or shut to provide shade
or privacy as required.

Flexibility is key to the design of the floating house, with the ability to open up or close down portions of the house with ease, depending on the weather and choice. Decks at the dockside provide a hinterland between the living spaces and the garden.

The main living space has a seating area at one end and a kitchen at the other (*left*); when the shutters are drawn back, it is flooded with natural light. The kitchen island doubles as a breakfast bar and dining table, and there is plenty of integrated storage close at hand (*above*).

The bedrooms are located on the lower level of the houseboat, which is partially below the waterline. Clerestory windows allow natural light to filter into these spaces, while preserving the waterproof qualities of the hull below window level; the bedrooms and bathrooms feature many bespoke, fitted and space-saving elements.

NEW CONCRETE HOUSE

WESPI DE MEURON ROMEO SANT'ABBONDIO, SWITZERLAND

Lake Maggiore is a startling intersection. It is where Italy meets Switzerland, the mountains meet the water, and a gentle, almost Mediterranean climate rubs up against snowy Alpine peaks. Here, on the Swiss side of the border, on the lower slopes of Monte Gambarogno, architects Wespi de Meuron Romeo have created a house that makes the most of the views. From this vantage point, the water is spread out before the towns and villages inhabiting the opposite shore, with the rugged peaks of the Bosco di Remo towering behind. The city of Locarno lies a little further north, towards the tip of the lake.

The three-storey house was commissioned by the clients as a holiday home, although it may well be used as their main residence in the future. The building is pushed into the steep slope of the hillside, accessed from a roadway that sits below the house. A slim series of steps, bordered by grass, ascend from a parking area alongside the road to the house itself, which has a crisp, box-like geometry. Yet the use of materials and texture, openings and apertures, intersections and enigmas, lends this concrete box a depth of character and interest, as well as framing a series of different views and vistas of the dramatic natural surroundings.

A key element of the house's enigmatic character is established by the use of concrete. The slim timber boards used to hold the concrete in place during construction have left a patina on the surface of the house, with the grain and knots of the wood, as well as the outline of the boards, clearly visible on the façade. It lends the building an organic, natural finish, combined with the monumentality of the concrete box. Inside, natural materials are also used to contrast with the concrete finishes, including stone for floors and outside spaces and oak for bespoke joinery, including doors, panelling and furniture.

The three-level house occupies a commanding position on a hillside overlooking Lake Maggiore. The upper level features a sequence of integrated outdoor rooms and terraces woven into the rectangular outline of the building.

The lower two levels are devoted to the bedrooms — minimalist spaces arranged around the irregular window openings — which include large apertures focused on the lake and the opposite bank. The main living spaces are arranged in an open plan on the top floor, which naturally has the best of the light and the views. The multi-functional kitchen, dining and sitting area is bordered by a partially sheltered courtyard, which sits in the neat outline of the building.

'The idea of the upper floor is to have one continuous space for everyday living,' says architect Jérôme de Meuron. 'It feels like an outdoor space, with huge sliding doors that can be drawn across in the wintertime when it's cold. The courtyard is a typical outdoor space, which offers protection and shade, but the walls around it are also an important light reflector, as the house is orientated towards the north to the view of the lake, but the sun comes from the back.'

The main sitting area is positioned alongside the largest window in the house, a floor-to-ceiling wall of glass that offers a panoramic view of the lake and the Alpine scenery. The vista is drawn into the house itself, along with the fresh mountain air from the courtyard. Up on the roof, there is an additional outdoor space: a substantial roof deck, bordered by glass balconies, with a herb garden planted to one side, placed between the openings to the courtyard on the level below.

The house takes a familiar form and a familiar idea — the building as a pure piece of geometry — and then, through its many textures, tricks and turns, creates something altogether more unexpected, original and engaging, enhanced throughout by the constant connections with the water and the mountains.

GROUND-FLOOR PLAN

FIRST-FLOOR PLAN

SECOND-FLOOR PLAN

The timber used to hold the concrete in place during construction has left a patina on the surface of the house (*opposite*). The window openings are irregular, framing particular aspects of the vista (*above*).

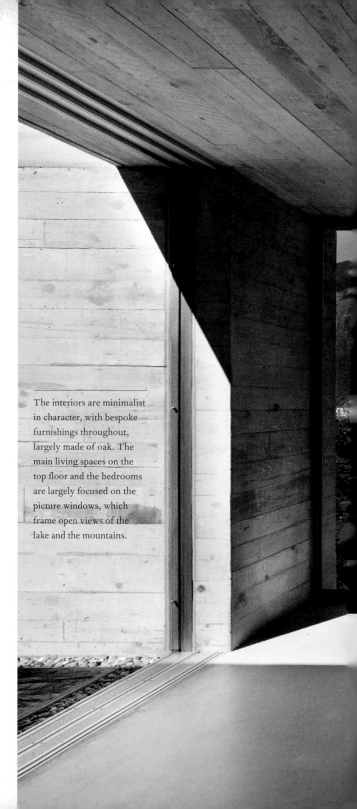

The interiors are minimalist in character, with bespoke furnishings throughout, largely made of oak. The main living spaces on the top floor and the bedrooms are largely focused on the picture windows, which frame open views of the lake and the mountains.

The house provides a choice of
integrated outdoor spaces, with a large
roof terrace at the top of the house –
featuring a timber deck and herb garden
– and a more sheltered run of terraces
on the floor below, positioned alongside
the main living spaces.

PENCALENICK HOUSE

SETH STEIN ARCHITECTS FOWEY, CORNWALL, UK

Pencalenick is a house of substance, rich in character and texture. With seven bedrooms and generously proportioned living spaces, it is also a house of substantial scale, yet manages to mitigate its presence on the landscape with a sensitive and considered design philosophy.

Approaching by road, along narrow lanes with high hedges and blind bends, is a mysterious process, as the house never fully reveals itself, even as you draw close. The building turns its back on the surrounding woodland, despite its beauty, in favour of a view out across the water. Arrival by boat is a more satisfying experience. The house sits on the shores of Pont Pill creek and looks out across the mouth of the River Fowey towards the picturesque town of Fowey itself; the estuary is used for mooring sailing boats, adding to the cinematic quality of the setting. Arriving over the water from the town, the glass and timber façade of the two-storey house comes into focus.

Surrounded by 1.6 hectares (4 acres) of oak woodland, Pencalenick was once the site of a Victorian hospital for patients in quarantine. The hospital was largely in ruins by the time it was discovered by property developer Johnny Sandelson, who commissioned architect Seth Stein to design a new holiday home here for himself and his family. The house is now also rented out for part of the year to holiday-makers.

The planning process was helped by the precedent established by the crumbling hospital buildings and the promise of restoration for the site and its surroundings. The discretion of the design was also in its favour, with the building tucked into the landscape. Outdoor terraces are positioned on the upper level, while a long balcony serves the sequence of bedrooms on the upper storey; substantial glazing throughout makes the most of the views out across the creek and river.

The house is tucked discreetly into the hillside, facing the creek and the town of Fowey across the water, and is accessed via a sloping stone jetty. The mature woodland around the house provides both privacy and intimacy.

'The house is just one room deep, so everyone gets to enjoy that vista,' says Stein. 'To go with the view, we wanted large, glazed panels, many of which are fixed in place, so the issue of natural ventilation is resolved by louvre panels in red cedar. These can be opened up or shut, depending on who is using the space, giving animation to the façade.'

The circulation spaces of the house are pushed to the rear of the building, where long spinal corridors run parallel to the concrete retaining wall, pressed against the hillside. A long skylight set into the grass roof brings natural light into the back of the house and draws it right down to the lower level via a frosted glass bridge, which spans the double-height sitting room on the upper storey.

Apart from this concrete spine, the rest of the house is constructed with a laminated timber frame, delivered to the site in prefabricated modules, as well as glass and stone. Local slate finds expression in the sitting room in the form of a crafted wall that intersects the middle of the house at a diagonal, forming a dramatic surround for the fireplace, and continues out onto the terrace, where it becomes a visual echo of the angled jetty leading down to the water's edge.

Surrounded by National Trust woodland and set within such a sheltered and unique setting, the house has a truly escapist quality. 'It is such a fantastic site, and the building manages to create a lot of interest through some very simple ideas,' says Stein. 'There is no doubt that when you go to the house, it always feels very special. It is a very calm place from which to contemplate the world.'

FLOOR PLAN

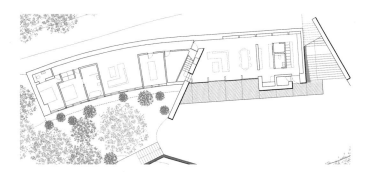

The house is pushed gently into the site, facing the water, with a grass roof to lessen the visual impact even further (*opposite*). A circulation corridor sits to the rear of the building (*above*), lit by a skylight.

The living and dining areas sit within a double-height space at the heart of the house, with the kitchen to one side (*above*). The seating is arranged around a wall of slate (*right*), which projects outwards from the front of the building to help bookend the terrace and frame the view of the creek.

The green grass roof creates an enigmatic approach to the house from the rear (*above*); a long skylight slices into the roof and illuminates the circulation corridor below (*above right*). Bedrooms and bathrooms on the upper level (*right and opposite*) benefit from elevated views of the woods and the water, as well as access to the balcony, with fresh air provided by the timber louvres.

THE PIERRE

OLSON KUNDIG ARCHITECTS LOPEZ ISLAND, WASHINGTON, USA

Nestling into a rocky outcrop on a rugged coastline, The Pierre offers an extraordinary contrast between mass and transparency. Sitting within the San Juan Islands, in the borderland between the US and Canada, the house is slotted into the rock itself with certain parts of the building characterized by a raw, cave-like quality. This crafted home also seeks a powerful and intimate relationship with its surroundings, with banks of glass framing a striking view of the water and coastal landscape.

'The contrast between mass and transparency was the principal driver for the design,' says architect Tom Kundig. 'The mass and solidity of the rock becomes the yin to the transparency of the house, which becomes the yang. I wanted the nature of the site to dominate.'

The client has owned the property for many years, and turned to Kundig to create both a retreat and a backdrop for her collections of art and furniture. The rocky outcrop was always her favourite spot on the site, with an elevated position and an open vista of the water and woodland to the rear. The decision to place the house within the rocks drew upon the example of cave dwellings in Italy, Turkey, Mali and other parts of the world, but also upon the rural vernacular tradition of leaving the most fertile part of a site free for planting, and building on the most stable and least productive portion of the land.

'The decision to truly engage with the site and the rock was a natural evolution of that idea,' says Kundig. 'That led to building the house in the rock and using crushed stone, quarried out as aggregate, for the flooring, and using larger boulders to build a garage. The site is certainly incredible, situated on a wonderful bay with the Salish Sea beyond. The house responds to the very human desire to be able to survey your surroundings while feeling safe.'

The single-storey building nestles among the rocks overlooking the waters of the San Juan Islands. The house has a green roof, further reducing its visual impact on the site.

The building is entered via a narrow alleyway that was partly cut into the rock, creating a somewhat processional entrance. This entry area is bordered by a small powder room with a particularly cave-like quality, with sunlight provided only by a light tube drilled into the ceiling. The entrance sequence is sheltered by an internal wall of recycled timber, which also hides utility spaces behind pivoting bookshelves, and emerges from the rear of the house in the form of a crafted timber storage pod.

The majority of the house is on a single level, with the living spaces arranged in an open plan. The main living area is at the heart of the floor plan, sitting on an axis that runs right through the rocky outcrop, with walls of glass at the front and back. This space has been zoned with areas devoted to the kitchen/breakfast area, a dining table at the centre and a seating zone placed for the best of the views. It opens onto a partially sheltered terrace, complete with an outdoor fireplace; the base of the hearth is formed from another stump of rock. A master suite sits to one side, with a modest guest bedroom alongside; another guest room is on a lower level.

In some respects, The Pierre recalls the work of modernist masters such as John Lautner, whose Elrod House (1968) in Palm Springs, California, was famously woven into a rocky cliffside, with boulders that edge into the house itself. Yet Lautner built on a grand scale, with tectonic bravado. The Pierre is a more modest building in every sense, conceived with great sensitivity to the landscape and respect for the natural context. For a building created on a relatively small scale, it has a powerful sense of depth and resonance.

A fireplace on a terrace carved out of the rock makes this an outdoor room for all seasons (*opposite*). The concrete and glass create a contrast with the rounded contours of the surrounding stone (*above right*).

LOWER GROUND-FLOOR PLAN

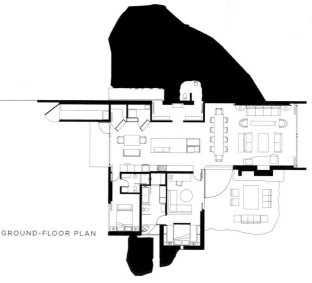

GROUND-FLOOR PLAN

The main living spaces are arranged in an open-plan sequence, and culminate in a seating area arranged around a fireplace with a stone hearth as well as the view of the water. The lighting fixtures were inspired by the work of Seattle-based interior designer Irene McGowan.

The interiors combine an eclectic mix of furniture, lighting and art with raw finishes and bespoke touches, such as the fireplace (*opposite*, *bottom right*) and kitchen (*above*). An internal wall made of textured, recycled timber (*left*) shelters the entry hallway and conceals utility spaces.

The natural rock edges its way into the house, appearing in its raw state in the powder room (*above*) and bathroom (*right*), where the rock itself serves as a wash basin. The master bedroom (*opposite*) flows out onto the terrace and enjoys a powerful view of the water, framed by the stone outcrops.

TOUR ALL SONER

TANIA URVOIS DOUARNENEZ, BRITTANY, FRANCE

The Urvois family share a particular love of the ocean. It lies behind the history and design of a house on the Brittany coast that is a considered response to a dramatic site, overlooking the Bay of Douarnenez. Here, architect Tania Urvois designed a house for her parents that makes the most of the sea vista and forms a discreet presence on the clifftops, tucked into the hillside and partly sheltered by pine trees. The house combines a semi-transparent pavilion on the upper level with more private sleeping quarters on the lower storey; both layers form a powerful relationship with the ocean view.

The house is a few miles from the coastal port of Douarnenez, a town of considerable charm with a working dock. The architect's father Louis spent his childhood here, and his own parents were fishmongers in the town. After ten years of searching for a suitable site on which to build a coastal home, Louis and his wife Kersti came across a small and undistinguished Breton house, owned by a local family, built in the 1970s and surrounded by mature trees and planting.

'My father wanted a house with a view over the ocean, so he waited a long time,' says Urvois. 'The irony is that the original house, which had a typical whitewashed façade, was more visible from the bay than the new house. Now the glass reflects the pine trees, which makes the house disappear. It is very discreet.'

Urvois studied in Spain, England and the US, and has worked in the atelier of Spanish architect Rafael Moneo. When the opportunity arose to design and build the new family home at Douarnenez, Urvois settled in Brittany, where she founded her own architectural practice and also teaches at the School of Fine Arts in Brest. The house took some years to design, guide through the planning process and construct.

The house sits upon a bluff overlooking the bay (*opposite*). Expanses of glass lend a strong degree of transparency to the upper level of the house (*below*) and enhance the sense of connection with the water and the natural surroundings.

Urvois drew inspiration from Mies van der Rohe's Farnsworth House (1951) and Philip Johnson's Glass House (1949), designing the upper level as a glass pavilion. The interior is largely open plan, with a fireplace offering subtle separation between the main seating and dining areas at the front of the house. The kitchen to the rear is also semi-open plan, with modest utility spaces tucked away by the entrance area; a slate floor helps unify the entire space. The kitchen and interiors were created in collaboration with the architect's sister Claudia, an interior designer.

The lower storey, tucked into the hillside, received a very different design treatment. Here, a media room, gym and garage are pushed to the enclosed rear of the lower-ground level. A sequence of five bedrooms sit side by side at the front of the house, all framing views of the ocean and the trees. Materials are more earthy and organic, with oak floors and many integrated elements made in timber.

'My parents wanted the maximum amount of light and had no issues with privacy, so I wanted to find a solution that was liveable and practical,' says Urvois. 'Rather than having a sheer, uncompromising form of architecture, we created a balance between the open living and dining spaces and the bedrooms downstairs, which are much more private. There is quite a contrast between the two storeys.'

Tour All Soner is now a home that is enjoyed by the whole family. Louis and Kersti Urvois spend the summer months here, and their children join them periodically. It is a place where the ocean can be enjoyed to the full: sailing, waterskiing, scuba diving and spear-fishing. And the house itself offers the perfect vantage point for appreciating the changing rhythms of the sea.

FIRST-FLOOR PLAN

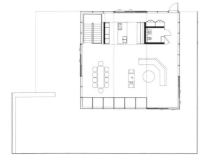

GROUND-FLOOR PLAN

The building is arranged over two levels, with a sequence of bedrooms on the lower storey. The upper level contains the main living spaces within a transparent glass pavilion, bordered by terraces.

A monolithic fireplace wall in the living space on the upper level partially separates the dining and seating areas, while the kitchen sits to the rear. The sofa is by Poltrona Frau and the dining table is a bespoke piece by Claudia Urvois, with Hans J. Wegner dining chairs.

Bedrooms on the lower level have floor-to-ceiling windows that frame the vista of the trees and the sea; the sliding glass walls also retract to offer fluid connection with the deck at the front of the building.

LAKESHORE SENTOSA HOUSE

BEDMAR & SHI SENTOSA, SINGAPORE

Lakeshore Sentosa House represents an extraordinary fusion of
international influences. Architect Ernesto Bedmar is Argentinian by
birth and training, and came to Singapore, where he based his practice,
via South Africa and Hong Kong. His clients, Katie Page and Gerry
Harvey, head an international retail empire in Australia with interests
across Asia. Sentosa itself, an island resort sitting off the Singapore
mainland, combines Asian and western ways of living.

The house forges a strong relationship with the water and outdoor
living in a multitude of ways. It sits on the edge of a lagoon, which
threads its way through this gated enclave, while a long swimming
pool sits at one side of the house, with a fish pond by the entrance. This
creates three different waterside elements, which at times seem to blur
and combine with one another when seen from particular perspectives.

'The relationship between the house and the water is a very
important one,' says Bedmar. 'Living in Sentosa means being close
to the water, so we designed the living-dining area, plus a study, at
the top of the house to gain views of the lagoon as much as possible.
The pond at the entrance and the pool by the side are elements closely
related to tropical living. They provide a psychological idea of coolness,
and a container for water plants, lilies and lotus, which are very much
associated with the culture and tropical climate of Southeast Asia.'

The clients, says Bedmar, wanted a simple, practical and elegant
house with a direct relationship with the lagoon. One of the key points
of inspiration was the boathouse typology, while the overhanging pitch
roof is reminiscent of Malay long houses and useful for dealing with
tropical rains. At the same time, the house is decidedly contemporary
and combines clean lines, large amounts of glass (which help dissolve

A lagoon, with private boat moorings and docks,
provides a waterside backdrop for the house
(*opposite*); the main living spaces are on the upper
storey to make the most of these views (*below*).

the boundaries between inside and out) and teak, which lends a real sense of organic warmth to the building.

Placing the main living spaces at the top of the house creates a strong vantage point that makes the most of the views out across the water. The kitchen, dining area and sitting room are open plan, with a large, elevated terrace beyond, from which a spiral staircase in sculpted steel descends to the garden below. Walls of glass slide back to bring a fresh breeze to the living areas, while a second, floating terrace cantilevers out over the pool and offers a degree of shade. A mezzanine level makes the most of the high ceiling heights in the upper portion of the house, and contains a large study with a more intimate seating area.

The lower level is devoted to the master suite, which faces the lagoon, and two guest bedrooms. The main entrance to the rear is accessed via stone steps, which float over the fish pond. The rear elevation is more enclosed, providing privacy from neighbouring buildings, yet the indoor-outdoor relationship is fully enhanced in all other parts of the house, with the master suite flowing out to a terrace. Natural cross-ventilation cools the building, and the use of sustainable timber is another key component of the environmental strategy.

'The timber shutters are one of the elements that pleases me most,' says Bedmar. 'The house can be 100 per cent open or closed, depending on the needs of the owners. These needs might relate to the temperature and climate, but also to privacy. And when no one is staying in the house, the shutters come down and keep the building secure. It's part of the simplicity and practicality of the house.'

FIRST-FLOOR PLAN

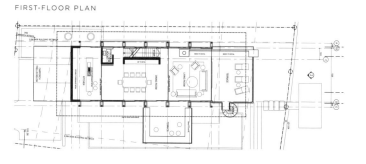

A steel spiral staircase provides an external link between the elevated terraces on the upper storey and the decks around the pool on the ground floor; the cantilevered, projecting terraces also provide shelter and shade for the outdoor rooms below.

The main living area on the upper level offers a fluid sense of connection with the terrace alongside, while the mezzanine holds a study area; the sofas are from Flexform and the chairs from Cassina.

The pool echoes the smooth surface of the lagoon and creates a mirror, reflecting the trees and sky (*opposite and above*). Bedrooms and bathrooms are located on the lower level (*left and above left*), which has a greater level of enclosure and privacy – although even these more intimate spaces offer connections to the decks and pool.

MAISON D

LODE ARCHITECTURE QUIMPER, BRITTANY, FRANCE

The relationship between Maison D and the water is a subtle one. Mature trees surround the house, which sits in a rural location not far from Quimper, and provide a natural camouflage, as well as a sense of privacy and intimacy. The tidal estuary of the River Odet is nearby, yet the water and moored boats in the channel are only glimpsed through the trees. The owner, who first got to know the region during childhood holidays, wanted a riverside home, but finding a suitable site was difficult. Eventually he fell in love with this special spot by the Odet.

'The area is protected, so it is a challenge to build something new here,' says architect Arnaud Lacoste. 'It took some time to get planning permission. We had to work within a height restriction and the plan of the house is right at the limit of the area that we could build on. The owner wanted a very simple cabin, but we pushed for something a little bit bigger and with a greater sense of connection with the landscape.'

The character of the house was shaped partly by the twin roles the client wanted it to play in his life: that of a private retreat and of a welcoming home in which he could entertain family and friends in an informal setting. The result is a building of two levels, each with a very different function and identity. The sociable ground floor is largely open plan, with floor-to-ceiling glass to the front and sides, creating a fluid sense of connection with the surrounding terraces and greenery and those edited glimpses of the river. Luserna stone has been used for the internal floors and the terraces to help the flow between inside and out.

The main seating area to one side is arranged around a suspended, floating fireplace. The kitchen and dining area to the other are anchored around a bespoke kitchen island, made of chestnut wood. The island is one of many specially designed fitted elements, as is the staircase that

Lush planting and mature trees provide a natural green filter between the house and the river; the timber cladding on the upper level reinforces the organic link between the architecture and the setting.

sits at the middle of the floor plan. The stairs are contained within a latticed timber box, which forms a sculptural and enigmatic feature at the heart of the building.

More functional and utilitarian spaces are pushed to the rear and tucked into the hillside that rises at the back of the house. The upper level has a very different quality altogether, with two large bedrooms and a study with a more enclosed and intimate quality. A brise soleil, also in chestnut, wraps the entire floor, lending it more organic, cabin-like connotations. The brise soleil continues around the windows and two integrated terraces, creating a sense of continuity and cohesion.

The twin terraces also serve as light boxes for the floor below, with large side windows looking down on the lower storey and offering some sense of connection between the two levels. From the upper storey, and particularly the roof terraces, which adjoin the two bedrooms, there is the notion of a double filter to the waterside views, which are glimpsed through the brise soleil and the trees beyond.

Maison D is a house of two distinct parts, but with a series of carefully composed connections. They have different but complementary relationships with the natural surroundings and the River Odet.

'We liked the idea of seeing the river between the trees,' says Lacoste. 'It's not an obvious link, but more of a mood, with these framed glimpses of the water. The owner bought the site because of the natural setting, so of course we didn't want it to feel at all urban. It is a house in the woods, with these openings to the river.'

FIRST-FLOOR PLAN

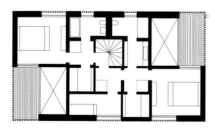

GROUND-FLOOR PLAN

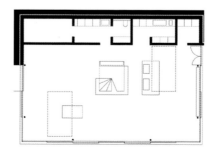

The house is pushed into the gentle slope, with services to the rear. The living areas are on the lower level; above are the bedrooms and roof decks, recessed within the rectangular outline of the building.

The River Odet offers both moorings and a navigable passageway to the sea, used by a range of yachts and larger ships. The planting provides privacy and enclosure for the house, with edited glimpses of the water.

The main living spaces are largely open plan and revolve around the view, a fireplace and the bespoke staircase and its enclosure at the heart of the plan. Sliding glass walls offer easy access to the terraces and provide a constant link with the green surroundings; the sofas are from SCP.

The dining area and kitchen are lightly and partially separated from the seating area by the staircase and its custom surround. The kitchen and dining table are bespoke, while the dining chairs are by Thonet.

DIRECTORY

JONATHAN ADLER

Seaside House, pp. 34–43
333 Hudson Street, 7th Floor,
New York, New York 10013, USA
jonathanadler.com

BATES MASI ARCHITECTS

Genius Loci, pp. 108–15
138 Main Street,
Sag Harbor, New York 11963, USA
batesmasi.com

BEDMAR & SHI

Lakeshore Sentosa House, pp. 236–43
12a Keong Saik Road,
Singapore 089119
bedmarandshi.com

BERNARDES ARQUITETURA

Casa MTL, pp. 66–75
Rua Corcovado, 250, Jardim Botânico,
Rio de Janeiro, Brazil
Rua Iramaia, 105, Jardim Europa,
São Paulo, Brazil
bernardesarq.com.br

PIET BOON

Kas Dorrie, pp. 44–55;
Floating Home, pp. 188–99
Skoon 78,
1511 HV Oostzaan, Netherlands
pietboon.com / pietboonbonaire.com

DUANGRIT BUNNAG

EV06 House, pp. 144–51
41/1–2 The Jam Factory,
Charoen Nakhon Road,
Khlong San, Bangkok 10600,
Thailand
duangritbunnag.com / dbalp.com

BURLEY KATON HALLIDAY

Whale Beach House, pp. 168–75
46a Macleay Street,
Potts Point, New South Wales 2011,
Australia
bkh.com.au

CADAVAL & SOLÀ-MORALES

Oport1 House, pp. 98–107
Avenir #1 ppal 1a,
08006 Barcelona, Spain
ca-so.com

WALLACE E. CUNNINGHAM

Crescent House, pp. 176–85
P.O. Box 371493,
San Diego, California 92137, USA
wallacecunningham.com

FEARON HAY ARCHITECTS

Dune House, pp. 14–23
P.O. Box 90-311, Victoria Street West,
Auckland 1142, New Zealand
fearonhay.com

CARLOS FERRATER

House for a Photographer II, pp. 76–87
Balmes 145 Bajos,
08008 Barcelona, Spain
ferrater.com

JORDI GARCÉS

Silver House, pp. 116–25
C/ d'en Quintana 4, 2n 1a,
08002 Barcelona, Spain
jordigarces.com

**GRAY ORGANSCHI
ARCHITECTURE**

Seaside House, pp. 34–43
35 Crown Street,
New Haven, Connecticut 06510, USA
grayorganschi.com

To Brian and Margaret

The authors would like to express their particular thanks
and gratitude to all of the architects and designers
who have helped to make this book possible and to the
many homeowners who assisted us and showed us such
generous hospitality on our travels. We would also like
to thank the following: Faith Bradbury, Gaby Hanrath,
Karin Meyn, Danielle Miller, David Nicholls, Richard
Pike, Neale Whitaker and Gordon Wise. We would also
like to express our gratitude to Karen McCartney for her
generous assistance.

Thanks are also due to all at Thames & Hudson for
their support and encouragement, particularly Lucas
Dietrich, Elain McAlpine and Adélia Sabatini, and to
Anna Perotti.

All plans and drawings supplied by the architects.

On the cover: *Front* Palais Bulles, Antti Lovag;
Back, clockwise from top left Cap d'Antibes House,
KallosTurin (first two photos); Oport1 House, Cadaval
& Solà-Morales (third and fifth photos); Experimental
Station, Johnson Naylor; Ocean House, Robert Mills;
Kas Dorrie, Piet Boon; Altamira Residence, Marmol
Radziner; House for a Photographer II, Carlos Ferrater;
Palais Bulles, Antti Lovag; New Concrete House,
Wespi de Meuron Romeo; Silver House, Jordi Garcés

First published in 2015 in hardcover in the United
States of America by Thames & Hudson Inc.,
500 Fifth Avenue, New York, New York 10110

thamesandhudsonusa.com

Library of Congress Catalog Card Number 2015932476

ISBN 978-0-500-51800-7

Printed and bound in China by Shanghai Offset
Printing Products Ltd